Across the House

The Art and Science of World Universities Championship Debating

Ian T. Lising

University of La Verne

Kendall Hunt

publishing company

Cover images provided by the author.

Kendall Hunt
publishing company

www.kendallhunt.com
Send all inquiries to:
4050 Westmark Drive
Dubuque, IA 52004-1840

Copyright © 2010 by Kendall Hunt Publishing Company

ISBN 978-0-7575-7410-8

Printed in the United States of America
10 9 8 7 6 5 4 3 2 1

Contents

Foreword

Quite simply, Ian Lising is the best person to write a book on the art and science of World Universities Debating Championship (Worlds) debating. His involvement with Worlds spans 20 years as a debater, judge, coach, and administrator. In that time, Worlds changed considerably in the way debates are conducted and judged. It also changed as an institution and as a community. As a senior member of the Worlds community, only Ian can describe those changes and give the reader a sense of why Worlds debating is the way it is. Readers will benefit from Ian's unique perspective.

The history of Worlds can arguably be divided into two periods: 1981 to 1996 (early Worlds) and 1997 until today (modern Worlds). What marks the transition between these two eras was a period of significant and sustained regulatory reform that would change Worlds forever. These changes included:

- Mandating four-team parliamentary debate as the standard format for Worlds (previously, the format and rules of debate were determined by the host institution).
- Agreeing on a set of Rules that covered how debates were to be conducted and judged (these Rules were only possible once the format of the tournament was standardized).
- Introducing oral adjudications (previously, debaters did not receive any formal feedback after debates).
- Allowing Worlds to be hosted for the first time by Asian, African, and Eastern European universities.

These reforms directly and indirectly changed the way in which Worlds debates were conducted and judged. The Rules focused debaters and adjudicators on a range of objective criteria. Oral adjudications increased the accountability of judges and the learning outcomes of debaters. One result was a new thirst for debate know-how that books like *Across the House* seek to quench.

Taking the competition to new regions encouraged the debut of countless universities that suddenly found themselves proximate to the most exciting and competitive form of parliamentary debate in the world. Students from new nations engaged external coaches and faculty coaches and demonstrated a commitment to learning about parliamentary debate that made many experienced Worlds debaters and adjudicators take notice. Again, students and coaches new to debating yearn for more information and guidance. *Across the House* is a comprehensive and clear guide that they will welcome.

Usually change brings some unintended consequences too—and some that not all would think desirable. Today, some experienced coaches and adjudicators are concerned about whether manner is given due consideration in modern Worlds. They observe that panel discussions are dominated by matter-related issues. If this is true, it is worrying. We know from communication and influence theory that the same adjudicators are almost certainly persuaded and influenced by effective manner, whether they discuss it or not. Yet by not dedicating a substantial part of the panel discussion to it, adjudicators may make manner conclusions based on their own biases and heuristics.

If these concerns are valid, then this book is timely. It deals with manner in a very comprehensive and thoughtful way. The book provides many practical tips, detailed explanations, and useful analogies for understanding the impact of manner and improving presentation skills. Ian's Worlds experience is telling as he skillfully addresses manner nuances associated with debaters coming together from different cultures.

One other inclusion I would draw attention is the (good) decision to include method as a separate part in this book, even though it is not a separate part of the Rules. The Rules borrowed aspects of method from Australian debating. Specific method concepts such as organization of arguments, consistency in argumentation, and debate dynamics were secreted under the headings of matter and manner, largely for political reasons. Sensibly, with first-hand knowledge of the Rules drafting process and his experience of Australian debating, Ian has made method a focus of this book.

This book is a demonstration of Ian's Worlds journey: a boy attracted to high school debate in America; a young man who led the emergence of the Philippines onto the world debating stage and fell in love with European and Australian styles of debate; and now, a man who has dedicated his life's work to developing his students and the Worlds community. Like Worlds, Ian's journey has more chapters to be written.

Ray D'Cruz
August 24, 2009
Melbourne, Australia

About the Author

Ian Lising received his B.A. in Political Science from the Ateneo de Manila University in the Philippines. He received his M.A. in Education from the University of La Verne. He was a lecturer and Debate Coach of the Ateneo from 1994–1998. He also taught at the Ateneo High School from 1994–1997 and at the Assumption College from 1997–1998. He began coaching the ULV Forensics Team in the fall of 1999 and started teaching Speech Communication in 2000.

Professor Lising was the co-founder, chair, and coach of the Ateneo Debate Society from 1991–1998. He coached Ateneo to win the Asian Debate Championships at the inaugural event in 1995. In 1998, Ateneo was the first Filipino team ever to qualify for the World Quarterfinals. In 1999, he served as the Championship Director of the Worlds Universities Debating Championships (WUDC).

In September 1999, he took over as the Debate Coach of the University of La Verne. He led his team to the Grand Final of the 1999 Oxford Union International Intervarsity Debating Championship and the Grand Finals of the 2000 WUDC in Sydney. At the 2001 WUDC in Glasgow, La Verne advanced to the World Semifinals. In 2003, the La Verne was the only U.S. university to advance past the preliminary rounds of the WUDC. In 2007, La Verne won the United States Universities National Debating Championships.

He is a six-time Grand Finals Adjudicator at the World University Debating Championships. He served as the World Debate Council Chair from 2002–2008. He was honored with the World Debate Council Order of Distinction and named World Council Member Emeritus in 2008. At the University of La Verne, he teaches argumentation and debate, results-oriented interviewing, public controversy and criticism, and rhetorical theory.

Acknowledgments

If one's life can be summarized by words on a page, it should really be just a long list of names. This book is actually the product of many years of sacrifice, love, and support that the menagerie of family and friends blessed me with throughout my life. It is to them that I owe the deepest debt of gratitude and dedicate this book:

My beautiful wife Lissa; my son Quino; Pop and Mom; my brother Dino and his wife Mylene; my sisters Amanda and Kathryn; my cousins, aunts, uncles, nephews, and nieces from the Lising, Tanseco, and Leung families; my grandparents; the Bernardo Family; Ray D'Cruz; Ning Achacoso-Sevilla; Dr. Jeanne Flora; BXC; Dr. Omar Salahuddin; Mr. John Bjorklun; Fr. Richard Leonard; Dr. Susan Evangelista; John Long; Ben Richards; Jeremy Brier; Neill Harvey-Smith; Andy Hume; Meg O'Sullivan; Colm Flynn; John Meany; Derek Lande; Taufik Albar; Kevin Massie; Praba Ganesan; Steve Johnson; Carel Nolte; Tim Skrastins; JJ Rodriguez; Sean Krispinsky; Drew Kim; Rob Ruiz; Josh Martin; Henry Nuñez; the administration, faculty, staff, and students of the University of La Verne; President Steve Morgan; Dr. John Gingrich; Dr. George Keeler; Dr. Rita Thakur; Dr. Jerome Garcia; Andoni Albert; Marc Abaya; my former colleagues and students at the Ateneo De Manila High School and University; the ULV Debate Team; the Ateneo Debate Society; my friends at the Oxford Union; Monash Association of Debaters; the Sydney Union; University College Dublin; Cambridge Union; University College Cork; Yale Debate Association; Hart House; and finally to all of the students that I have yet the honor to instruct.

CHAPTER 1

Introduction

Human conversation has rarely prioritized the need to be accurate over the incessant need to simply be "right." The basic desire to be believed and understood has and will always dominate the immediate communication agenda. People want to say what they want to say precisely when they want to say it, without reservation or remorse. This is typically achieved with little or no regard to either strategic planning or effective outcome. However, ever since people first started flirting with their own brand of unique ideas, there have always been people just waiting to contradict them.

Debating served as the proverbial fly in the ointment long before the hateful rant of the misinformed talk radio program, the permanently raised hand of the know-it-all sitting in front of the classroom, or the long-winded meanderings of the colorful guest at cocktail parties. As the cavalcade of thoughts parade well past the point of our general interest, we often feel the urge to say just the perfect thing to "put them in their place" and genuinely shut them up. The ability to combat the myopic pontification from a misguided soul has always had universal appeal, and as purposed by this book, is achievable by all.

The formalized activity that debating has evolved into this century is really no different at the base level. From coffee house convos to the seemingly endless constellation of blogs, we discuss issues ranging to the latest hot-button topics buzzing through Capitol Hill to the mindless drivel that always seems to define Hollywood. But the forum to engage these issues with the most balance and purpose will always be the debating chamber.

As part of classical education, formal debating provided the rhetorical forum for students to hone their communication and critical-thinking skills. Over time, many schools watered down the practice to intermittent elocution contests or relegated the task of learning how to argue to simple writing exercises in composition classes. Whether due to financial cutbacks or changes in pedagogy, debate took a back seat to other academic disciplines. In the United States, it has even disappeared completely from several curricula.

Recently, this trend seems to be reversing. Over the past few years, especially in other nations across the globe, academic debating has been experiencing resurgence. Regional, national, and international tournaments are steadily growing in number and participation. Fledgling programs are now scrambling for materials and guidelines to train with. Unfortunately, there are well over a dozen different formats used for competitive debating. This makes it rather difficult to navigate the particulars of the activity.

During the very first World Debating Championships ("Universities" was added to the name of the event later on), it was decided that the host institution would determine the format for the tournament. This would mean that when the tournament was hosted by the United States or Canada, it would be held in the American Parliamentary format. For every other host nation, the British Parliamentary format was employed. This led to massive judging inconsistencies and much frustration with the experience. At the Cork Worlds 1996, the World Debate Council decided to codify the British Parliamentary format as the official format used for all future World Championships. Ray D'Cruz was tasked to write the rules that were first used at the 1997 Worlds in Stellenbosch. These have been the official rules of the Championships and have been in use ever since.

This does not, however, explain why the Worlds format should be worthy of your own industry and investment. This perhaps can best be described from a personal perspective. My first exposure to competitive debating was in Kearney High School, in Kearney, Nebraska. I was a member of the National Forensics League, and I competed in Policy, Mock Trial, and Student Congress. "Speed" debating was all the rage at the time. The concept of debating in that fashion was to inundate your opponents with as much material as possible, making it hopelessly impossible for them to respond in kind. This was being celebrated and practiced by all of our competitors and recognized by all of the judges.

Our coach, Mr. John Bjorklun, forbade us from doing the same. He was an old school coach and always quipped, "The *quality* of argumentation must always be prioritized over its *quantity*." He refused for us to engage in speed debating and knew full well that the speed judges would always certainly hand us the loss. As frustrating as it was to lose all the time, we believed in his philosophy and knew that we were debating the "right" way.

I attended my undergrad studies at the Ateneo de Manila University in the Philippines. The debating landscape in the Philippines was rather curious. They competed in a format they referred to as "Oregon-Oxford." I later found out that in the early half of the 1900s, the University of Oregon and Oxford University held a debate friendly. Since they couldn't agree on the format, they created one. This format was somehow adopted by the visiting American educators in the Philippines and took root throughout the country.

When Ferdinand Marcos declared martial law in 1972, competitive debates were extremely limited. One could argue that encouraging the youth to rally the people behind radical ideas in a public debate would not be in the best interest of a dictatorship. Rather than having tournaments, annual showcase debates were held. When Marcos was deposed in 1986, debating slowly found its way back into practice.

As freshmen, Ning Achacoso and I were part of the team that defeated Ateneo's archrival De La Salle University. On the heels of our victory, we founded the Ateneo Debate Society. Given my Policy and Ning's Oregon-Oxford background, we toyed around with hybrid formats and approaches. It was during our sophomore year that we received an invitation from Trinity College Dublin for the 1992 World Debating Championship. We were the only Filipino institution at Worlds. We were so excited to attend the event, but we had no clue what to expect. What we found was exactly what we were looking for.

Suffice it to say that having to experience your very first British Parliamentary debate during a round that you are actually competing in is quite daunting. What made it worse was that we faced Oxford A during our very first round. Despite our lack of experience in BP, we found that the format celebrated the best parts of what we always thought debating should be. This allowed us to perform beyond our wildest expectations.

What we discovered was that the BP format was so much more dynamic and allowed for innovation otherwise punished by other formats. The motions were extemporaneous and forced us to have a broad understanding of not just one subject matter, but all. Points of information kept our minds tangoing with more dexterity than we ever thought possible. Extending cases from closing positions required us to be creative and flexible. Immediate rebuttal reminded us to vigilantly maintain relevance. We knew immediately that we had to share this experience with everyone.

It is from that very spirit that this book is written. This is not only meant to be a foundation for those who are new to the activity or format, also a guide to those who advanced their debating and adjudicating careers as well. By no means am I claiming that this book is the panacea for your debating ills. It is designed to help you cultivate your own ideas and marshal them into poignant expression that will persuade, motivate and captivate. It will help you understand how to translate these skills beyond the debating chamber. Who knows? You might even win a few rounds along the way.

The title of this book, ***Across the House***, actually comes from an old school form of cheering on your competitor in the greatest display of sportsmanship possible. Since this is a simulation of debating at a house of parliament, all in attendance are considered members of the House. The House is divided into two parts, the Government and Opposition. These sit on converse ends of the debate floor facing each other.

The gulf that separated members of the House is considered to be "uncrossable." In theory, if you cross the House, you are crossing political party lines. As heated as debates get, the only acceptable moment to "cross the House" would be at the conclusion of the round as a sign of respect for the other side and to make clear that nothing said in the debate was meant to be personal. This would mean that the debaters would come to the middle of the floor and shake hands and exchange pleasantries. This was the only part of the debating culture that remains totally intact.

Saying "Across the House" during a debate round is never done anymore. Actually, this was rare even during my debating days. This was a compliment paid by any debater from the other side of the House during your speech. As you will learn in Chapter 12, there are other means of doing this for speakers from your side of the House. However, doing the same thing for speakers from the side opposite only seems insincere and may even be misunderstood for mocking. This should never be confused with saying "cross the House." Asking someone to cross the House is actually a mocking phrase that is pointing the contradiction in a person's speech. In other words they are saying, "You might as well just cross the House, since you seem to agree with us." This confusion was another reason why people use neither phrase currently.

By actually saying "Across the House," you are actually giving applause and congratulations "from across the House" or from the other side of the House for a great point, argument, or piece of evidence. This was hardly used because it seemed like a sign of weakness or general concession. I always felt it was much like watching a competitor do something amazing in a sporting event and wanting to show your appreciation for it at the very moment you witness it. Some might think that it would only highlight just how phenomenal the argument was and influence the judge to give them the win right then and there. But if a debater is confident in his or her own ability, this would only motivate that person to do better. Debaters would strive to hear a few "Across the House" compliments during their own speeches.

This book is divided into three separate sections: **Matter**, **Manner**, and **Method**. These are the three criteria of debate first defined by the Australian Debating Federation. These were later outlined and adopted by the Australasian Debating Championships. Ray D'Cruz incorporated key concepts of these criteria to the WUDC rules. While Matter and Manner remained intact in the final set of WUDC rules, Method was retained in principle, subsumed into the other two criteria. However, I chose to discuss Method separately in this book for clarity and specificity. The next chapter, **The Debate**, will take you through the entire process of a round.

Additionally, I have included the *WUDC Rules*, the *Guide to Chairing and Adjudicating a Worlds Debate*, and the *Guide to Bidding, Planning, and Running a World Universities Debating Championship*. All of the documents are officially adopted by the World Universities Debating Council and are incorporated in this book so that you will get a complete picture of how to debate, adjudicate, and even run you very own tournament.

As you can most probably tell by now, my approach to debating (and education as a whole for that matter) is really quite unique. Over time, I have developed this philosophy and woven it into all of my instruction. My personal pedagogy has been defined by three core maxims:

1. **Debating brings the best and worst out of the best and worst people.**

   Debating teaches you to utilize and maximize facets of your mind and personality that you never knew existed. Being able to tap into your potential and discover abilities you never thought belonged to you is quite an amazing and exhilarating experience. You may have once thought to yourself, "I never care about the news," then one day find yourself scouring through news sources and wonder how this happened to you. You may think that you have no original opinions and feel that it be best not to get involved, but then find your blood boiling because of something someone said to you in a random casual conversation.

This also means that the better you get at this activity, the more dangerous you can potentially become. It is important to remember that the skills that you learn, hone, and perfect along the way can be extremely destructive when used with the wrong intentions. Skills can win you a round, but they never define your character. The power to persuade is quite seductive and easily corrupts the wielder. After all, Adolf Hitler is often renowned as one of the greatest speakers of all time. Debate is the activity that helps us become more resolute in our actions and, more importantly, to understand our reasons for doing them.

2. **Great debaters are not born, but made.**

   To paraphrase the philosophy of a fictitious chef from a recent computer animated cinema classic, "Anyone can debate." I have trained so many people who would claim that they could never stand up in front of an audience. Others wore shocked expressions when I told them that they would be delivering seven-minute speeches. But not too long after a few sessions, those same students would whine about not having *enough* time to have their say. Don't get me wrong. Of course there are people who are simply naturally gifted. And, yes, it comes easy to them and they do exceptionally well. But I've also seen them annihilated by those who maximized the little potential they had to start with.

3. **The best dishes are off menu and have no precise recipe.**

   It may be a little ironic that I mention this in a textbook, but there is absolutely no *singular* method to success in debate. They are as varied as the eyes that read these words. This is the reason why my debaters find great success but never at the cost of who they were, are, and hope to be. I may give them the field to play on, the basic rules of the game, even a few plays to call. But once it starts, the game is truly their own.

   Debaters are not robots that you just plug and play. They are not parrots that just repeat everything their coaches tell them to say. They are not replicas of the successful debaters that have come before them or facsimiles of the institutions that they represent. They are unique and the approach necessary to capture their true potential should be just as unique.

This book is designed specifically with these maxims in mind. I just hope that this book serves as tool as you work your way through the exciting and challenging adventures that debating often provides. So get ready to load matter, sharpen wit, open minds, and do what is most important—enjoy the round.

CHAPTER 2

The Debate

Set-up 1:

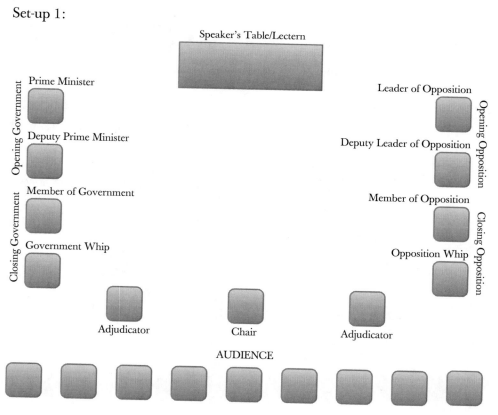

Speaker's Table/Lectern

Prime Minister

Opening Government

Deputy Prime Minister

Member of Government

Closing Government

Government Whip

Leader of Opposition

Opening Opposition

Deputy Leader of Opposition

Member of Opposition

Closing Opposition

Opposition Whip

Adjudicator

Chair

Adjudicator

AUDIENCE

Set-up 2:

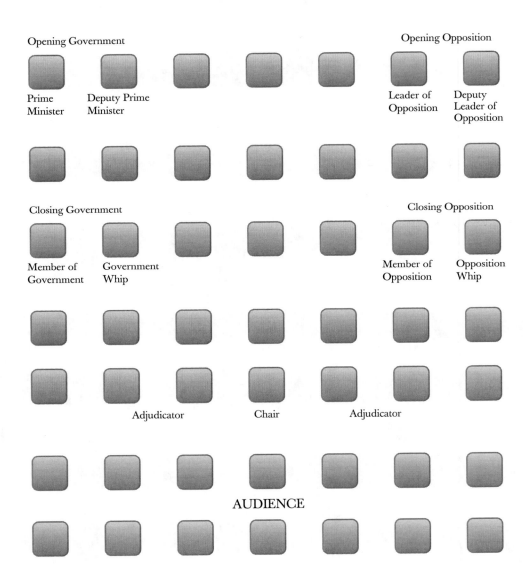

Set-up 3:

Speaker's Lectern

Closing
Government

Opening
Government

Opening
Opposition

Closing
Opposition

Adjudication Panel

AUDIENCE

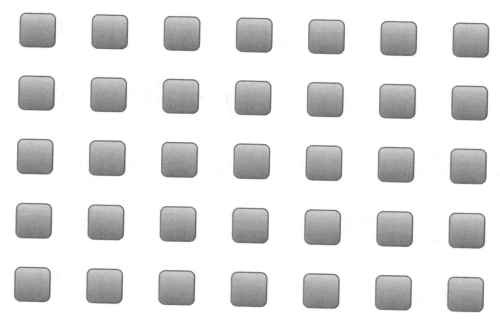

A World Universities Debating Championship formatted debate round starts at a briefing room. This room is typically a large lecture hall (or auditorium for tournaments) that has enough room for debaters (speakers), adjudicators (judges), and observers (public audience). Debates should normally be open to the public, which would mean larger crowds at the elimination rounds and finals of major tournaments. Some tournaments will feature debater training and orientation as well as a separate adjudication briefing and accreditation exam. At larger events, adjudicators are actually briefed in a separate room altogether.

Each team will consist of two debaters. Intervarsity (IV) competitions may include more than one team per institution. The team members are not interchangeable with other members of their contingent. So teams must have the same partners throughout the IV. The teams are typically lettered to distinguish one from the other. So, if three teams were debating from the University of La Verne, the teams would be La Verne A, La Verne B, and La Verne C.

A Worlds format debate round features four teams in each debate round. The tournament organizers will first randomly assign teams to different rooms matched up against one another. They will then post this on an electronic projection on a big screen, an overhead projection, or several printed copies taped to the wall of the briefing room. This is referred to as the *pairings* or the *draw*. Each team will be assigned into one of four positions: Opening Government, Opening Opposition, Closing Government, and Closing Opposition.

The adjudicators are also assigned to rooms in odd-numbered panels of at least three. A chair is designated from the panel for each room. At tournaments, there should be no conflicts between the adjudicators and any of the debaters in that room. Conflicts are any relational characteristic that would cause undue bias for or against any team. This would include institutional conflicts (being from the same university), coaching conflicts (if the adjudicator spent any extensive time coaching the competitor in the recent past), and personal conflicts (romantic or personal relationships that would render questionable the adjudicator's objectivity). At smaller events where there are fewer means to avoid the conflicts, these conflicts must be prioritized, and at desperate times permitted. The typical way to get through this is to balance the bias as much as possible. For example, if there were four institutions represented in a round, a panel of five would include one adjudicator from each institution and a neutral chair.

Once all of the debaters and adjudicators know which rooms they are assigned to and what positions they will take in the round, the motion is released. The motion is the idea, philosophy, and/or policy up for debate. It is also referred to as the resolution. It is erroneously called the topic. This is not the case since a topic is quite general whereas a motion requires much more specificity. The motion is projected on a screen and read out to the debaters. Where screen projection is not available, all participants should have access to a printed version to avoid misunderstandings with the syntax.

The Government teams are tasked with supporting the motion and the Opposition are meant to, well, oppose it. The Closing teams are there to extend the debate by using new perspectives or enhancing the previously presented arguments from the Opening teams with unique development. This simulates the phenomenon in Parliament or Congress when members may support an issue, but not come from the same political party. For example, a Democrat would typically support the right to choose in an abortion debate, whereas a Republican would defend the right to life. But if a Republican supported the right to choose, he would want to speak on the issue, but separately from the Democrats since they only agree in principle but have different ways of approaching the issue. This feature of the Worlds format is what makes it truly unique and academically challenging.

After the motion is release, the debaters have 15 minutes to prepare with their partner prior to arriving at the designated room. They are not permitted to prepare or engage in motion-related conversation with anyone aside from their partner. They are also disallowed from accessing information through any electronic device. So laptops, iPhones, Blackberries, mobile phones, or any similar devices are to remain switched off until the very end of the debate.

At some point before the debate begins, the debaters should decide what speaking order they will follow. There are eight speakers in each round. Each speaker has a unique role and function to fulfill in a debate round. These are outlined in much greater detail in Chapters 5 through 8. During the debate they will speak in this order:

1. Prime Minister (Opening Government)
2. Leader of Opposition (Opening Opposition)
3. Deputy Prime Minister (Opening Government)
4. Deputy Leader of Opposition (Opening Opposition)
5. Member of Government (Closing Government)
6. Member of Opposition (Closing Opposition)
7. Government Whip (Closing Government)
8. Opposition Whip (Closing Opposition)

Adjudicators are permitted to enter their designated room at any time after the motion was released. However, the Opening Government is the only team that has the option of using the designated room for its preparation. If they are indeed in the room, the adjudicators should afford them the opportunity to work in private and enter with the rest of the teams as soon as the 15 minutes have elapsed.

As the teams situate themselves in the room, they should follow Set-up 1 if they are in a room that has movable chairs or benches. The tournament organizers should have previously set up the room, but if not, face the Government seats across their Opposition counterparts. There should be an empty space (as much as possible) between the two sides. The Opening teams should be further upstage with the Closing teams closer to the adjudication panel and audience. The Government should always be seated to the left side of the room and the Opposition to the right just like the actual Parliament.

If the room is a lecture hall or has fixed seats, the participants should use Set-up 2. Since they are immovable, choosing seats in the general vicinity of the designated area for each team is sufficient. Unlike Set-up 1, everyone is forced to face forward. The Closing teams should sit behind the Opening teams and skip rows if possible. The audience should not be sitting anywhere near the competitors in Set-up 2. The audience also should always leave the area designated for the adjudicators' seats vacant and give as much room as the adjudicators require.

Set-up 3 is used for finals at major IVs. Generally reserved for theaters and grand halls, the elevated stage would include all the debaters sitting as teams at designated tables. The adjudication panel, which is considerably larger depending on the tournament, will sit together on one long table off stage (on the floor with the audience) facing the debaters.

The Chair of the adjudication panel will begin the debate by calling the House to "order." This means that everybody should remain silent. This will be discussed in more detail in Chapter 12. The Chair will say something to the effect of, "On the motion 'This House supports a nationalized health care system,' I call this House to order. I now welcome the Prime Minister, Ms. Jane Chan from University X, to speak on behalf of the motion that stands in her name." The Chair will use variations of this for every speech that follows. "We thank the honorable Prime Minister for her speech and now welcome the Leader of Opposition, Mr. Mohammad Smith from ACME College, to open the case for the opposition benches," or "We thank the honorable Member of Opposition and invite the Government Whip, Amit de la Cruz from Galaxy Tech College, to conclude the case for that side of the House."

Every debater is allotted seven minutes to speak. There are other IVs that run five-minute speeches during preliminary rounds. But Worlds format is strictly seven minutes. The time begins when the speaker chooses to start speaking. It ends when the timekeeper (usually the Chair of the adjudication panel) indicates. The speaker is given a brief grace period (10–20 seconds) with which to conclude her speech. This is not to be abused. Time begins when the speaker starts speaking.

The first and last minute of the speech are protected, which means that they cannot be interrupted. To indicate the protected time, a bell is rung, table knocked, or gavel banged by the timekeeper at the end of the first minute and before the start of the last minute of the speech. The signal is given twice (i.e., two rings, knocks, or bangs) at the end of the last minute. The timekeeper should give the signal thrice if the speaker exceeds the grace period.

During a debater's speech, between the end of the first minute and last minutes of his or her speech, any debater from the side opposite **is** permitted to offer *points of information*. This means that if the Prime Minister is speaking, the Leader of Opposition, Deputy Leader of Opposition, Member of Opposition, and Opposition Whip may offer a point of information. If the Member of Opposition is speaking, the Prime Minister, Deputy Prime Minister, Member of Government, and Government Whip may offer a point of information. A debater's partner or any other member may *not* offer points of information from the same side of the House.

To offer a point of information, a speaker rises at any time during the unprotected time of the opponent's speech. A debater has the option to accept the offered point or refuse and politely sit the opponent down. Taking too many points of information would limit the amount of time that a debater is leaving for his or her own speech; taking too few makes the person look like a coward. Two to three points of information are expected during a seven-minute speech. If the debater accepts an offered point, he has effectively yielded the floor to his competitor for a brief amount of time. Points of information are any *question* or *statement* provided by the debater to an opponent. These are not to exceed 15 seconds. More details about points of information are included in Chapter 12.

Each debater is invited to the floor by the chair in the correct sequence. At the conclusion of the round, the chair invites the members to "cross the House" or to shake hands. As the debate is now concluded, the chair invites the members to leave the debating chamber. This is when the adjudication panel conducts its deliberation. When panel members finish, the debaters are called back into the room and the result is revealed to them by the chair. The teams are ranked first through fourth. Speaker scores are not to be revealed to the debaters, however. The chair will then explain the rationale for the decision. Afterwards, the chair welcomes any clarification that any of the debaters require. If the debaters wish to hear their advice about the round and possible strategies that they could have used, they may request this after the verbal adjudication is presented. This will make it clear to everyone that the suggestion/coaching advice was not the reason for decision. All adjudicators must only judge what the debaters gave them and not what they wished the debate to be or thought that it should have played out. The Adjudication Guideline will cover these and any other adjudication concerns you may have.

Finally, since the round is over, the debaters return to the briefing room to do this all over again. This time, however, the pairings will be done through power matching. This is a system that pits teams of similar records against one another. So, if a team received third in the first round, it will most likely face three other teams that also received third in their respective first-round debates. This process will keep going for as many preliminary rounds that an IV requires. At a 300+ team tournament like Worlds, there are nine preliminary rounds. At the end of the preliminary rounds, the top 32 teams are selected to compete in the Octofinal round. The elimination round then takes the top two teams in each round and advances them until the final. The Final will showcase the top four teams of the tournament, from which the champion is revealed.

PART I

CHAPTER 3

Matter

WORLDS' RULE 3.1 THE DEFINITION OF MATTER

3.1.1 Matter is the content of the speech. It is the arguments a debater uses to further his or her case and persuade the audience.

3.1.2 Matter includes arguments and reasoning, examples, case studies, facts, and any other material that attempts to further the case.

3.1.3 Matter includes positive (or substantive) material and rebuttal (arguments specifically aimed to refute the arguments of the opposing team(s)). Matter includes Points of Information.

Matter can best described as everything said, used, or referred to in a person's speech. This includes all the researched and referenced information, analogies, opinions, and thoughts that a speaker shares with the audience. This section will help the debater gather relevant material, understand the function of his or her speaking position, and construct his or her speech accordingly.

Debates can range from any issue that affects a local community to one that has implications on the global society at large. Some might try to categorize a debate as political, economic, sociological, ethical, philosophical, religious, or scientific, but will realize that several of their arguments will fall under a combination of those categories. The challenge is in discovering where all the pieces fit. So the question that most debaters ask usually comes in now, "Does this mean that I have to know everything?" This is actually partially true. The common perception that most people have of debaters is that they retain an impressive amount of information. No, this does not mean that all debaters will win on *Jeopardy!*, but they will generally be familiar with information pertinent to any topic of discussion.

POSITIVE AND NEGATIVE MATTER

Most of the time, people will deduce that debating is telling other people "they are wrong." This is in fact only half of the truth. Information used in a debate round could be classified as either positive matter or negative matter, depending upon how it is used by the debater. Positive matter is used to construct ideas that support the side of the motion assigned to a particular team. If a team builds a point, directs arguments, and provides evidence that create lines of logic that stand quite independently, then its matter may be construed as positive.

However, people usually enjoy attacking their opponents by criticizing what they have said. This material does not stand independently from the initial ideas that they are targeting. It is responsorial and is utilized completely with the purpose of addressing the substance constructed by their adversaries. This information is known as negative matter. It may be often referred to as *rebuttal* or *refutation* and will be discussed much more in later chapters.

The use of the material, therefore, dictates the fashion by which an audience can be influenced. In other words, it is not convincing enough for a team to prove that its opponents are wrong. It must equally set out to prove that independently of the opponents, that it is correct. If one person can prove she is right by simply saying that everyone else is wrong, then no one will ever be convinced of anything.

POINT, ARGUMENT, AND EVIDENCE

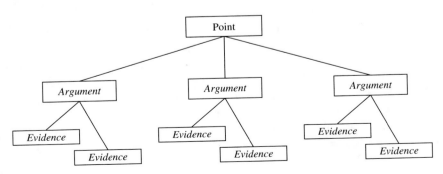

Most novice debaters would simply assume that spouting a tremendous amount of information would win them the round. The act of simply dumping as much material on the opposition as possible with the hope of burying them is facile indeed. It is absolutely critical that all debaters remember that the *quality* of matter exchanged in a debate round is always more important than its *quantity*.

An effective way of categorizing, and thereby utilizing, matter in a debate is to follow the point, argument, and evidence approach. All forms of speech must utilize these essential elements to make it effective. Many people try to make speeches without one or even two of these elements, rendering the speech pointless, senseless, or unsubstantiated. This will result in the speech lacking the credibility and coherence necessary for its efficacy.

Point

As simple as it might sound, a point is the central focus of a speech. Unfortunately, this becomes rarely utilized in conversational discussion, as people tend to favor a stream-of-consciousness form of discourse. Relative knowledge on a given subject might excite a novice debater to regurgitate everything that he might know about it, thinking that he will succeed with a hit-or-miss approach. Unfortunately, relevance to the important themes is lost, and the debater ends up missing the plot entirely.

The debater must analyze all the ideas that he has and organize them under the banner of a single point. This process may be a bit more difficult than it seems at first. The point should be a general overarching philosophy that guides the position that the team as a whole will support. It serves as the root for all the matter that the team will use throughout the entire debate. Australian debaters often refer to this as their *team line* or *theme*. The best way to approach this main idea is to try to simplify the philosophy in a single, uncomplicated sentence that clearly maintains the team's direction. This will be discussed in greater detail in Chapter 15.

Argument

The most common misnomer that people have about debate is to refer to it as "arguing." The reason for this is that arguments are indeed a great part of a debate round, but they should never be confused with being representative of the entire activity. An argument falls under the main point and connects it to a more specific idea. It is from here that a debater can provide reasoning behind the philosophy she created. The temptation to now jump off into a deluge of arguments is much greater, but a disciplined debater must exercise restraint. Two or three main arguments per speaker under the point she supports should be plenty. This way, the debater can spend more time fleshing out the argument, connecting it to the main point and the evidence that will follow.

Evidence

Worlds' Rule 1.3.3 Members are permitted to use printed or written material during preparation and during the debate. Printed material includes books, journals, newspapers, and other similar materials. The use of electronic equipment, with the exception of those that are exclusively dictionaries, is prohibited during preparation and in the debate.

Evidence is the material used to support the arguments used in a speech. Without substantiation, a speech relies too heavily on assertions to maintain integrity. The toughest thing about assertions is that they are quite easily shut down as speculative and inaccurate. This destroys the credibility of the speech (and the speaker, for that matter), and the round denigrates into a simplistic pageant of opinion. Evidence becomes vital as the "proof" that general statements can be based on, not the other way around.

Most debaters will inevitably create a series of "fact sheets" or an outlined file of pre-researched topic areas that may aid them during the debate round. Most of the time, this will only help if they have already initiated some degree of understanding the information previously. But building a library of information necessary to win a World Debating Championship will not come overnight. In fact, it will be the long-term commitment to acquiring information that will help not only in a possible career in competitive debating, but in life as a whole.

The process starts with dissecting the data into either of two compendia: **Regional Files** or **Basic Themes (First Principles)**.

Regional Files are rather simple to construct and provide an easier system to process and access. Files are first divided into seven parts: Oceania (Australia and the Pacific Islands), Asia, Europe, the Americas (North, South, and the Caribbean), Africa, the Middle East and International Organizations (UN, WTO, OIC, EU, ASEAN, etc.). Then, each file should be subdivided into six categories. These are historical, political, social, economic, religion/ethics, and science/medicine. Therefore, given a debate about possible presidential elections in Afghanistan, one only needs to access the political subsection in the Middle East file. Abortion in Indonesia? The religion/ethics subsection in the Asia file should be the best place for that.

Basic Themes or **First Principles** are more complicated to develop and should be utilized by debaters with a little more experience. The concept of "first principles" is boiling each debate down to the core principle by which the debate is hinged. This will permit the debaters to use the base principles that drive a specific topic that shares the same basic philosophies with another. When the themes are similar enough, the logic can be utilized by both concepts. For example, given the debate "This House supports the legalization of all drugs," a debater could develop the theme around *body autonomy*. Therefore, he may use similar justification points that are used to support the legalization of prostitution as well.

It is important to first pare down the complexities of the motion, leaving it with the fundamental root from which the debate can be prefaced. There are five first principles: Personal Freedoms, Identity Politics, Freedom Fighters, Nationalism, and Internationalism/Globalization.

Every person is born into this world with **Personal Freedoms**. These are thought to be inalienable, but are defined by social, economic, political, and cultural parameters. The general themes found here would be tenets outlined by the Universal Declaration of Human Rights, the Bill of Rights, or any other doctrine crafted to preserve individual liberties. Body autonomy, freedom of speech, the right to protect oneself, the freedom of movement, and crime and punishment are just a few examples of personal freedoms.

As individuals start to identify with others and wish to consolidate their freedoms, they engage in **Identity Politics** and define their own rights and organizational agenda. When people associate with others' given gender, sexual orientation, race, religion, economic status, or any other identity division, they may act as a group pursuing their collective needs and wants. The issues in this file would include women's equality, rights of the LGBT community, affirmative action, and prisoner's rights, for example.

As the individual association matures beyond specific identity politics, seeking recognition and control, but is met with resistance challenging his or her legitimacy, it is often referred to as a **Freedom Fighter**. Unfortunately, at times, associations are also handled with the considerably less desired label—terrorist. Sometimes, it's not as simple as finding a group and reducing its struggle to the question, "Well, what does it want?" This means that the research should include the historical context from which the organization was founded and thus the justification for its actions against the ruling class. The distinction between terrorists is additionally not as easy as simplifying it to "Well, they target civilians," or "They use fear as a tactic."

When the fighting is done, the freedom is won, and external regions recognize the people within their definable borders, they are usually recognized as a nation. The people embrace the tenets of their own **Nationalism** and protect their interests and the rights they wish to afford their citizens. This file includes topics such as immigration, cultural protectionism, use of a national language, and so on.

When nations wish to interact or cooperate with one or more other nations, **Internationalism** or **Globalization** is the goal. This is easy to identify, but difficult to navigate since the historical significance of the relationship between two or more nations will require the initial investigation. This file includes transnational/multinational corporations, international institutions (i.e., the UN, ASEAN, WTO, APEC), and bilateral/multilateral agreements.

Access to information is the next essential step. With the advent of the Internet, the sheer volume of information available at literally fingertips is both a blessing and a curse. It may seem overwhelming if people consider that they are about to embark on the quest to learn "everything." But the focus should begin by identifying issues circulating around current events. Each issue can now be categorized in the corresponding file one at a time. International debaters often refer to this practice as *matter loading*. The extemporaneous nature of this form of debate requires the debater to be able to understand the focus of the motion, determine the point of controversy, and recall all the information that he or she previously gathered that is pertinent to the issue in a very short span of time. The process is simplified if the debater is familiar with the material that she has researched. In other words, it is not recommended that debaters use information that they did not research, read, or fully understand on their own. This does not mean, however, that *all* information on a given subject *should* be used in a debate. Worlds Rule 3.2.1 states "Matter should be relevant, logical, and consistent." This simply means that debaters should utilize only pertinent information during a debate round.

Most of the time, there will be elements of the information that will be unfamiliar to the debaters. This may require them to research the historical background about the people, places, or events that are discussed in the current issue. For example, reading the current events about the Palestine–Israel conflict might lead to a comment made about Yitzhak Rabin. Rabin, the great political figure who was assassinated in 1995, may not seem relevant to the current issue, but further research will certainly prove otherwise. This simply means that matter loading does not end with reading the newspaper or watching CNN. It is simply the gateway to a lifetime of learning. Once the debaters find themselves comfortable with the general current events from the news, they will be ready for any motion that comes their way.

CHAPTER 4

Motions

WORLDS' RULE 1.2 THE MOTION

1.2.1 The motion should be unambiguously worded and give a clear indication of the intended general direction of the debate.

1.2.2 The motion should reflect that the World Universities Debating Championship is an international tournament.

1.2.3 The members should debate the motion in the spirit of the motion and the tournament.

Every debate must have a motion (or resolution). Without a motion, one may simply find himself at a chaotic and meaningless stream of consciousness convention. Since this format of debate is extemporaneous, understanding the motion becomes the first crucial objective. The debate round begins with four teams of two people being assigned to one of the positions discussed later in this section. Then, as soon as the teams have their respective positions, a motion is released. The debate begins 15 minutes after the motion is given. Each team uses the 15-minute preparation period to determine its strategy and outline its speeches. Without a clear motion, this could simply be a waste of their time. A more detailed discussion of preparation time will be addressed relevant to each team's role in the succeeding four chapters.

Since this form of debating is a simulation of a parliament, motions begin with the phrase, "This House." The purpose of the wording is to have the *government* side of the issue generally take the position of action against the status quo. This would naturally put the *opposition* side generally on the side that would support the status quo, thus negating the proposition of the government. Certain motions might implicitly place a government team on the side of the status quo, but that would entirely depend on the definition.

The biggest misconception that people have is that a motion is the same thing as a topic. The difference between the two is that a topic gives a person a broad range of ideas to work with, whereas a motion narrows the ideas down to a more recognizable focus. For example, if a debater were given the topic "death penalty," she would not know if she was meant to be for or against it. This gets even more complicated given that she is in a debate round. One team could possibly be prepared to speak about "the methods of capital punishment" and another could be ready for a discussion on "the historical impacts of the death penalty." Having spent 15 minutes on each "position" would in this case have been in vain. There would be no clear clash or position had this debate taken place. So a motion should be clearly stated to ensure a solid and balanced debate.

However, the clarification does not end here. Unfortunately, not all motions take the same form. There are two ways that motions are worded, the *open* motion and the *closed* motion. Of these, the preferred type of motion at international competitions is the closed motion. But from time to time, the other may rear its ugly head.

The *open* or *metaphorical* motion is worded in such a way that requires the most amount of interpretation. This means that the Opening Government is given a free rein to connect the debate to whatever it chooses to link it to. This is often seen as an unfair advantage for the Opening Government as the 15-minute preparation time becomes a waste for the other three teams. This also means that all of the strategy time for the Opening Opposition comes *during* the Prime Minister's speech. This type of motion is most commonly used when a championship committee becomes less than industrious or runs out of ideas.

A typical open motion might sound like, "This House feels lucky" or "This House supports life." A debater could link either motion to the death penalty issue: "Mr. /Madame Chair, the motion before the House this morning states that this House feels lucky. Well, indeed, Ladies and Gentlemen, we are all lucky to be alive. This is why we choose to protect the lives of all our citizens, which is why we reject the death penalty."

Unfortunately, the opposition speakers are not privy to the logical mindset of that particular debater. Furthermore, since they are not allowed to sit in with the Opening Government (or any other) team during the preparation period, they would just have to wait for the Prime Minister's speech to find out what they would talk about. Therefore, an open motion debate typically will lead to an Opening Government bringing up *canned cases* to an extemporaneous debate.

A *canned* or *pet* case is a government-positioned case that is prepared days, weeks, or in some instances even months before a debate is held. The immediate problem with this is not just the lack of fairness to the Opening Opposition team as mentioned earlier, but the matter used in the round will almost certainly be knowledge specific to months of advanced research on that specific issue. This usually ends up narrowing the debate in such a way that the clash over issues gets lost along the way.

A *closed* motion is worded in a way that requires the least amount of interpretation from the debaters. Given the motion, "This House rejects the death penalty in developed nations," debaters will know precisely what the content of their speech is and can anticipate the direction of their opponents. This gives the most fair amount of preparation for all the teams competing at a round. The fewer amounts of interpretation necessary, the clearer and more competitive the debate will be.

Most people would suggest that there are motions that are naturally biased for one side or another—that being on the Government side on the motion "This House supports the development nuclear weapons" would be patently unfair from the beginning. This assumption is wrong. The point of every debate is to see *both* sides of *every* issue. The debater must be able to defend the issue as fervently on the side opposite his or her personal beliefs as on the side that supports them. The goal of every debate is to celebrate diversity of opinion, belief, and understanding. Social dogma often limits a person's ability to formulate creative critiques on current views and practices. Debate forces these "abnormal" perspectives to the forefront and challenges blind devotion to popular pedagogy.

So, the person who thought that there is no argument that would make the support of nuclear weapons feasible may be looking at it from a developed nation's perspective. But the following argument can be made: "If the developed nations were built through the exploitation of developing countries with the power of nuclear weapons threatening them, isn't it time that developing nations that have now caught up with technology have the right to harness the same type of power? Not according to the developed nations. This is what developed nations want—they want to have freedom to control others whose freedom they can and will in turn restrict. This is unfair and this is why developing nations should have the right to build a nuclear arsenal. Developing nations should be guaranteed every right to the process of advancement and power control that the other nations have enjoyed for generations."

As a part of the academic exercise, teams are not permitted to choose the position they wish to defend on a given motion. So, even before the motion is released, four teams of two people are assigned positions for the debate round. The next four chapters will discuss the approaches to each team designation, how to utilize the preparation time wisely, as well as the individual roles for all eight speakers.

CHAPTER 5

The Opening Government

In the following chapters, we will discuss the role/function and strategies of each of the four team positions in a debating round. We will also illustrate the role and strategies of each of the eight speaker positions. The first of the four teams in a debate round is called the **Opening Government**. It is comprised of two speakers, the Prime Minister and the Deputy Prime Minister.

The function of the Opening Government team is to provide the scope of the debate through a clearly articulated case while upholding their side of the motion. Within the allotted 15-minute preparation time, only the two members of the team are permitted to work with each other. Building an Opening Government case consists of *identifying the critical point of controversy* of the given motion, *crafting a reasonable definition*, and then developing the team line through *individual speaker roles*. Additionally, the Opening Government should consider the unique function of *narratives, impact, models,* and *concessions* from its side of the House.

POINT OF CONTROVERSY

Discovering the point of controversy in each debate round begins with identifying the inherent philosophical dichotomy of the given motion. In simpler terms, it means that teams should be able to "draw a line in the sand." The motion will undoubtedly establish the point of controversy in an overt fashion, clearly positioning the government team behind the ideas that would hold the statement to be true. But unfortunately, even this can be misappropriated. With the motion "This House would permit professional athletes to use performance-enhancing drugs," some might think that the point of controversy *could* be in the type of drugs being permitted. Others might suggest that the point *could* be found in the type of sport where the drugs are permitted. But neither is the *real issue*. Discussing types of drugs and/or sports may be important when sifting through arguments, or even evidence for the debate, but this does not help to establish the point. The point of controversy *should* simply be whether drugs should be permitted or not.

This distinction might seem subtle to some, but it works wonders in clarifying a potentially confusing debate round. For instance, if the Opening Government presented a case of why steroids should be permitted by the National Football League, then they leave ambiguity on the level of other drugs and other sports. This way, the debate becomes muddled. It limits the scope of the debate to the perspective of the Opening Government even before it starts discussion on its definition. The use of steroids in the NFL would be fabulous as an example, or even as part of an argument, but the heart of the debate really is found in the *principle* of the motion as a whole. But seeing it as *the* debate straight away narrows the debate to a specific example and ends up disregarding other potentially rich ideas.

The Opening Government team should work out the basic process of discussing, "What is the principle being supported by this motion?" or "What change in the status quo is this motion trying to accomplish?" Using these simple questions, it can proceed with establishing where it would stand on the motion as well as anticipate where its opponents will be. This whole process should take no longer than 30 seconds to 1 minute. The team is now ready to develop its definition.

DEFINITIONS

As a team starts to "draw a line in the sand," one might wonder if now would be a good time to establish a more favorable position for the team. The team might think that it would be wise if it made sure the line gave the opposition as little ground to work from and put them at a disadvantage from the beginning. This is the ultimate mistake that people make when coming up with a definition. Debaters think that they are playing it smart by putting their opponents on a more difficult position and that it proves to be an easy win. This is certainly not the case. All they end up with is a muddled round with a lower degree of clash and, most assuredly, a poorer debate than its potential.

A definition is merely meant to serve as the dividing line between teams such that they know exactly where they are coming from and they know where their opponents stand as well. With a closed motion, the Opening Government does little if much work at all in coming up with the definition. The clearer the motion, the less articulation is needed to define the status of their positions. The definition is supposed to just set up the debate round by creating the boundaries that would limit the scope of the round and provide a greater degree of clarity. However, this clarity is never to be mistaken for a strategic tool.

Another mistake that is commonly practiced for a variety of reasons is doing a word-by-word analysis. This was typically used for open motions to clarify just what the debate was going to be about. So the Opening Government would proceed to take each word in a motion and provide dictionary definitions for each word until it could extrapolate what it wanted to for its canned case. This is obviously unnecessary in the context of closed motion debating. But surprisingly, there are still some teams that will attempt this from time to time, along with some even more bizarre definitions.

According to the Official World Championship Rules, there are four official caveats to forming a definition. A definition may be challenged by an Opening Opposition team under these conditions.

Worlds' Rule 2.1.3 The definition must:

(a) have a clear and logical link to the motion—this means that an average reasonable person would accept the link made by the member between the motion and the definition (where there is no such link the definition is sometimes referred to as a "squirrel");

Squirrels are definitions that take the debate away from what is often referred to as the "spirit of the motion." One of the clearest violations of this was found at the 1998 World Championships on the motion "This House would put an immediate ban on land mines." One Opening Government team thought that it was being clever when they proceeded with the following definition:

"Well, we know that land mines are dangerous and cause death and injury to others. We also know that these are found on land. There is another thing that is potentially dangerous and found on land. It is the automobile. So this is why we define this debate to ban cars from our land immediately and to return to the use of horse-drawn carriages."

Some might consider this interpretation "cute," but to the three other teams in the round (and the adjudicators as well), it serves as the best example of bad form. The other teams were clearly ready to engage in what would have been a balanced and intriguing debate about the given topic. But instead, their preparation time had been wasted, and now they faced a debate that had presumably been set in motion to their disadvantage. This is unacceptable. Not only was the spirit of motion abandoned, but also it was done in such an outrageous fashion that it insulted basic logic and intelligence.

Teams out of desperation often use squirrels. They find themselves with a motion that they possibly have no information or understanding about. So they proceed to shoehorn in a canned case by changing the parameters of the motion. In a very real way, teams that prefer open motions to closed ones feel that by utilizing this tactic, their abuse would be permitted. Unfortunately for them, and fortunately for fairness and good debating, squirrels are strictly forbidden.

(b) not be self-proving—a definition is self-proving when the case is that something should or should not be done and there is no reasonable rebuttal. A definition is may also be self-proving when the case is that a certain state of affairs exists or does not exist and there is no reasonable rebuttal (these definitions are sometimes referred to as "truisms").

Tautologies and/or Truisms are not as common in international debating as they once were, but they do manage to pop up from time to time. A tautology is is a statement that is true by its own definition. One simple way of looking at it would be to prove that A=A. In one debate round, a team was caught trying to define the motion that "The House would seek to reduce unemployment" in the following manner: "Members of this House, we will reduce unemployment by getting the unemployed people some jobs. This way, the numbers of unemployment will go down." As silly as this might seem, teams that attempt this type of definition typically have no malice in their action. But then again, they have no logical sense as well.

This should not be mistaken for the improper context that a debate might have given another particular circumstance. The 1992 World Championships featured the motion, "This House supports the right to strike." Many teams immediately complained that the status quo already protected the right. This was until they realized that some nations did not in fact recognize the right, or that in many nations, this was not extended to emergency service workers. This means that the definition can actually provide this bit of clarity to move the round into a "debatable" field of play. A truism, however, must not move the field of play once again into an unfair area and force the other teams into the realm of impossibility.

(c) not be time set—this means that the debate must take place in the present and that the definition cannot set the debate in the past or the future;

Time-set definitions are usually used to restrict the information in a debate round to one specific timeframe. This means that if an opening government is given the motion, "This House supports the censorship of the Internet," then proceeds to define it "some time in the year 2143 C.E., when technology has been perfected," then it would be quite clear that it is being quite unreasonable. Some teams might intentionally try to be clever and force people to debate positions in a purely theoretical and ungrounded assortment of wild assertions.

Other times, teams might try to use a historical perspective (i.e., This House would defend slavery in 1837) to gain an advantage.

There is an essential clarification to be made here. This does *not* mean that speculative information or historical input should be disregarded. The key idea here isn't so much that a debate can't be held to the standards of a time warp, it is that information used by other teams in the round that comes from outside the defined time period *should not be restricted* from the debate. So an Opening Government team may try and set up a debate in the past or future if it so desires, but it is forced to permit the other teams to destroy it by actually being relevant.

and (d) not be place set unfairly–this means that the definition cannot restrict the debate so narrowly to a particular geographical or political location that a participant of the tournament could not reasonably be expected to have knowledge of the place.

Place-set definitions are the most commonly misunderstood infractions of Worlds Rule 2.1.3 since teams often neglect the similar distinction made about time-set definitions. If a motion is defined in such a way that restricts examples or facts being drawn in from other places, then that is a place-set round. In other words, if the motion, "This House justifies the use of torture" is given to an Opening Government team, it may define it as "those captured and sent to the detention camp at the U.S. Naval Base in Guantánamo Bay in Cuba." But, if an Opposition team uses examples of prisoners from other places, the Government *cannot* claim, "but we are only talking about those in Cuba." The definition may therefore start as a jumping point to a much wider debate.

DEFINITIONAL CHALLENGES

Definitional Challenges are best avoided at all costs during a debate round. They are confusing and are not interesting in the least. The methodology of presenting a definitional challenge will be addressed when we discuss the Leader of Opposition's Speaker Role, but it is essential to note now that the proper care must be put into making sure that it never happens.

The easiest way to avoid a definitional challenge is to provide a definition that sets up a balanced debate. Debaters should ask themselves the question, "What position will this put the opposition in?" If they cannot answer the question, then they should try reframing the definition. A simpler way of looking at it is this: No team has ever legitimately won a single debate round in history by the way it defined a motion. But, on the other hand, countless teams with their "clever" or "tricky" definitions have lost not just their debate, but also all the respect in the world.

As much time is spent crafting a fair definition, it really shouldn't ever take much longer than two minutes. A good test to check if the definition is clear would be to have the debater practice delivering it to his or her teammate during the preparation time. The teammate could pretend to be an opposition speaker and see if the definition makes sense and provides enough ground. Once this is accomplished, the team should focus on the more important issues to best utilize its preparation time.

More time should be spent on developing the case that the team will provide for the rest of the debate. This entails outlining the main point or team line that the team came up with, branching the point off into precise arguments, and assigning the proper evidence to support each claim. Now, preparation time should be over and debaters should be ready for the round to proceed.

SPEAKER ROLES

The Prime Minister

The first to speak in the debate is the Prime Minister. There are three main roles that a debater must fulfill when in this speaking position: provide the **definition**, outline the **team's case**, and finally **develop positive matter** in support of the case.

In a seven-minute speech, a Prime Minister should spend no more than one minute to define the terms for the debate round. Since this should be a straightforward presentation; taking more than a minute would be a clear indication that the definition is faulty. The need for interpretation should have been eliminated, so using more than a minute to do so would be problematic. In fact, most advanced debaters in competition would spend under 30 seconds to get the definition out of the way.

It should be noted, however, that there are more artistic ways of presenting the definition rather than just blurting it out. The most concise way of doing this would be to provide the point of controversy, then the parameters of the round, and finally, the definition. This helps establish context for the other teams in the round and makes it abundantly clear just which direction the debate should go.

The next role for a Prime Minister is to outline the team's case. This task refers to the team line or philosophy of the Opening Government. Indicating to the audience this early on in the debate just what they should expect to hear from both the Prime Minister and Deputy Prime Minister would help clear the direction for the round and privy the adjudicators to the fundamental mindset that they should expect. This provides a solid foundation for the arguments that they will fill in as the round progresses.

Some debating circuits refer to this as "signposting" or "providing a roadmap." Some teams stylistically will not choose to outline the case in such a clear-cut fashion. They may simply imply through broader strokes just where the direction of their case will lie. This is acceptable but should be reserved for more advanced debaters. A novice speaker may have the tendency to lose him- or herself in his or her speech and potentially have the case stray too far.

It is also noteworthy for the Prime Minister to preview the main points of the Deputy. This will nuance the team cohesion and highlight the consistency between partners. This should not be carried too far, however, thus leaving the Deputy with a shell of a speech. The Prime Minister should provide nothing more than just subject headings or taglines that would serve as a notation of what positive matter to expect in the Deputy's speech. Elements for this should have been planned for during their preparation time.

All first speakers of every team (Prime Minister, Leader of Opposition, Members of Government, and Opposition) should avoid providing a *hung case*. These are cases in which the first speaker of the team provides a premise; a second premise is provided by the second speaker of the team; and only after the second premise is given may a conclusion be drawn. In other words, a team may not expect its opponents to follow its logical pattern without first completing the necessary conclusions first. If they don't provide the logical conclusion, they are leaving them "hanging" until the conclusion is drawn later. One example of this is on the motion, "This House would legalize drugs." If the Prime Minister sets out to prove that drugs exist in every nation in the world, and her partner will prove that these should all be legalized in the next speech from that team, then the end of the first speech proved nothing conclusive. This is therefore a hung case and is not permitted.

The Deputy Prime Minister

The Deputy Prime Minister is the second person to speak from the Government side of the House and the third speaker overall in the round following the Leader of Opposition. It is the Deputy Prime Minister's role to *rebut* the arguments of the Leader of Opposition and *develop positive matter* in support of the Government case, as promised by the Prime Minister.

A speaker in this position will have already heard the speech from the Leader of Opposition before he is called to the floor. This means that he needs to respond to the ideas forwarded by the Opening Opposition with rebuttal. Refutation or rebuttal is negative matter that is used to discredit and provide a direct clash with matter provided by the side opposite. But this also suggests that the Leader of Opposition would have provided a lot of rebuttal material targeting the Prime Minister's speech. So, the Deputy Prime Minister should also spend some time to deflect or attack the rebuttal material forward by the Opposition benches. Additionally, the Deputy Prime Minister should rebuild whatever the Opposition had damaged.

It would prove fairly disastrous if a Deputy Prime Minister simply abandoned what her partner forwarded in his speech owing to what the opponents brought to the round. At the same time, many debaters flinch at the suggestion that they come to the defense of an idea that was ridiculed just moments ago. The best approach that debaters should adhere to in this predicament is to revert back to the links that their team established from the team line. Simply put, if you get lost, go back to where you started from.

This way, rebuilding a case that had just been decimated does not end in frustration. In fact, it allows for a deeper understanding of the issues, given that the simple logic and background information would have already been established. Additionally, the context for the Deputy Prime Minister's speech allows for a more solid transition in response to questions arising from the Opposition.

The Deputy Prime Minister must rebuild what has been rebutted, refute the positive matter that the Leader of Opposition introduced, and provide the positive matter outlined by her partner. A speaker in this position should not only always remember to use her time efficiently, but must clarify any misunderstanding that might have suggested by the Opposition. If there are any definitional issues raised by the Leader of Opposition, it is the duty of the Deputy Prime Minister to set the record straight.

BUILDING THE NARRATIVE

Most debaters often forget that the activity is not held in a vacuum. They would present ideas to their audience under the preconceived notion that everyone knew exactly what they were talking about. Additionally, they forget that the audience did not have the opportunity to sit with their team during the preparation time. The common result of this is a jargon-laden speech that has no contextualization whatsoever. Additionally, the following speeches will equally have no grounding, further tangling the web of information spun by each speaker. The audience will be easily lost by the debaters, and the whole debate becomes an exercise of futility. This is the reason why debaters must embrace the concept of the narrative.

By its very definition, a narrative is exactly that, a story. But the difference with this story is that it most certainly has an antithetical telling. In other words, you will hear both sides of the story before the round concludes. Some think that this means that the Prime Minister should immediately tell the story, top to bottom, purely from the biased perspective of his side of the House. This is not the most ideal position to start the debate from. It will cue the audience into the tarnished mindset from the government benches without first feeling that they have a considerable hold on the issues involved.

The narrative should be built from the very basic level, which is particularly balanced. This neutral approach might seem like a waste of time, but it actually allows the audience in on the thought process. Any piece of information is, at its core, quite benign. It is the spin placed on the material that gives it positional substance. Therefore, the act of creating the forced perspective in the Prime Minister's speech must always follow a short and balanced framework.

In other words, telling a story from one perspective does not mean that the introduction of the setting and characters should be plotted out by a biased word. The first hint of partiality is much more effective if it comes later, as the audience is given the illusion of sorting out the material for themselves. Leading them directly to the conclusion that one character is good and the other evil is nowhere near as persuasive (or satisfying) as first introducing the characters in a balanced manner. Then, by introducing a brief series of events, only then is the audience allowed to "choose" which characters are the hero and villain.

Building the narrative, therefore, requires a little patience and timing. The Prime Minister could easily craft the first part of the definition with a brief, un-prejudiced contextualization then transition the last portion of the definition with the distinctly partisan government philosophy. This will provide the round with a solid base to start and works as a well-packaged definition.

The Deputy Prime Minister uses the framework created by the narrative to ensure that a cohesive line is maintained between the two opening government speakers. The more consistent the story appears, the more likely that teamwork will be rewarded. The new material introduced by the Deputy Prime Minister should be couched in terms that help the narrative along and should never infringe on the integrity of the Prime Minister's telling. It is most likely that if the neutral part of the narrative is crafted in a clear way, the opposition will not be required to rework any bit of it. In fact, a truly successful narrative will have a premise that will consistently be followed even until the Opposition Whip's speech. This will be the clearest indication that the tenet presented by the Opening Government is relevant and gives its team the best chance of being re-membered by the audience (and adjudicators) at the end of the round.

CREATING THE IMPACT

The power of ideas goes only as far as they can effectively transform the mind-set of those they are shared with. Information can be a pretty useless tool if its relevance and impact on the world are not channeled correctly. The marketplace of ideas is constantly flooded with half-baked and ill-conceived notions that bear little or no consequence to anyone involved. Impact is the crucial element that eludes many speakers who drown themselves in wave after pointless wave of in-formation with no insight as to how anything affects or is affected by everything else. Impact allows the debaters to engage the listeners with a palpable link from the conceptual to the actual.

Developing impact is critical to the analytical lines drawn out by the Opening Government and the sustainability of its case. This is approached in many ways, but it is recommended that the Prime Minister incorporate impact from the very beginning of the speech. She would start by drawing a mental pic-ture for the audience. Then, by enticing them to spot what is wrong with it, the status quo is defined and identified as the culprit, and the damage that is done to society can be clearly laid out. This gives the Opening Government the opportunity to explore the theoretical difference between the philosophy that she is formulating from her side of the House and that of the opposition.

USING MODELS

A common misperception about Opening Government teams is that they are bound by some rule to construct a case from their side of the House using a *model* or mechanism currently used by someone, somewhere in the world. First of all, though commonly used by convention by several regions and teams, it should be noted that the official rules of the World Championship do **not** mandate that a model must be part of a government case. It does, however, make a lot of sense when discussing broad, overarching themes and deep philosophical theories to explore them in a tangible example in the real world.

The problem with this is that Opening Government teams usually become complacent (or lazy) with the one example and tend to leave the debate shallow. So, the presentation lacks the depth of analysis, and the opening team thinks that by merely connecting the dots between its philosophy and the model, its job is done. If this is the case, then the Opening Opposition typically is satisfied with chipping away at the government case by only attacking the model. If Opening Opposition is successful with this, it is typically rewarded with "decimating" the Opening Government.

However, if multiple examples of the same philosophy are introduced, then the Opening Opposition is forced to attack the themes developed by the Opening Government. This deepens the debate and ensures that the Opening Government case will last further than simple model refutation by the Opening Opposition.

Finding the right model isn't about retrofitting current events situations into whatever broad themes the Opening Government decides to come up with. It works better to think of the principle that generates one side of the controversy and to drive the point through the model instead. This way, several models may be included—even historic ones. An example of this would be using the motion, "This House supports the sex trade industry." A Prime Minister might suggest, "Let's set this debate strictly using the Dutch model." If he chooses to do this, then nuances found in other models or projected policies could simplistically be left out of the discussion. But it would work far better if the Prime Minister suggested, "Let us support the idea that a woman or man should be permitted to use his or her body as desired. This was largely popularized by the Netherlands, but its acceptance is equally shared by many nations across the globe." This way, teams are not bogged down by too many particulars of the Dutch model specifically. Rather, they can spend a great deal more time supporting the principle from a variety of perspectives. They can also draw on the differing sex trade policies found in the UK, Australia, Asia, and even some states in the United States.

MAKING CONCESSIONS

Much like creating balance for the round when formulating the definition, the Government shouldn't be too quick to close all the loopholes that naturally exist given their side of the motion. It would seem instinctive to protect one's case with as many defensive barriers as a team can mount, but this may cut off deeper analysis that may actually win a round.

An example of this could be found in an abortion debate. This will certainly draw clear sides that even beginning debaters are aware of. One side will argue the merits of the "right to choose" as the other will defend the "right to life." If the right to life crusaders create their case in fear of what the other side will say, they will actually be limiting their own position. During preparation time, they might think to themselves, "Our opponents will say that a woman has the right to decide what to do with her body. So, let us argue that a woman does not have the right to control her body." This line of thinking will only place the team in a precarious position, one they may not be able to dig themselves out from.

Instead, the team should consider that, "Yes, it is true that a woman has the right to body autonomy. We will concede that right exists, should be protected, and is considered sacred. But this isn't a debate about just the potential mother. This debate is whether the woman's right to choose is more sacrosanct than potential life that depends on another." This way, the team not only appears to be more credible and balanced, but it is now not compelled to defend the notion that women do not have a right to control their bodies. This ends up moving the debate away from a position of control.

The concept of concession is more clearly understood with the metaphor of a chess match. It is correct to assume that one must read his or her opponent's move several steps ahead. This is absolutely critical in chess. However, if the moves are never actually made to bait the opponent, then the game can never begin in earnest. It is best for the player to sacrifice the pawns in order to get the more important pieces and positions on the board. Debate works in exactly the same way. A debater should be able to sacrifice some elements of his case in order to strategically set himself up for much more effective arguments and placing himself in clearer ground.

However, it should be make extremely clear that neither the philosophy nor the themes that personify a particular side of the House should ever be conceded by the side opposite. Teams should never waver back and forth when it comes to the foundation upon which the debate is founded. This will be discussed in more detail later in the section that covers *counter plans* and why they should never be used.

CHAPTER 6

The Opening Opposition

The second of the four teams in a debate round is called the **Opening Opposition**. It is comprised of two speakers, the Leader of Opposition and the Deputy Leader of Opposition. The function of the Opening Opposition team is to provide a clearly articulated case upholding its side of the motion and refute the case provided by the Opening Government. Within the allotted 15-minute preparation time, only the two members of the team are permitted to work with each other. Building an Opening Opposition case consists of *identifying the opposing perspective* of the given motion and then *fulfilling the individual speaker roles* accordingly. This chapter will also explain why opposition teams should never use "*counter models/plans.*"

AN OPPOSITION'S PERSPECTIVE

The preparation time of an Opening Opposition team is in part an act of creation inasmuch as it is an exercise in anticipation. It is never nearly enough for an opposition to simply negate the ideas of the Government then call it a day. The Opening Opposition should actually form an independent case, typically supporting the rationale of the status quo. The presumptive nature of foretelling a possible government case would give the Opening Opposition enough room to construct lines of argumentation that would serve as good rebuttal, but it shouldn't dictate the general direction of the opposition case.

Given the motion, "This House supports the criminalization of performance enhancing drugs," an Opening Opposition may presume that the Opening Government will run the case outlining the dangers of steroid use. So, it would seem obvious for the Opening Opposition to use the preparation time solely on refuting the claims on dangerous steroid use. However, this would be a superficial position, merely responding to the ideas as they are forwarded by the Prime Minister.

The more effective strategy would be to explore the rationale that athletes across the globe have benefited from other technology, independent from the ideas that steroids are safe. It allows the opposition to set up its own arguments that the Deputy Prime Minister and hopefully even the Closing Government will have to respond to. This will help the Opening Opposition place its concerns above mere rebuttal points and ease the introduction of its positive matter.

The Opposition Narrative is also important to build, just as it was for the government bench. The narrative is more than just the same story as told from the perspective of those affected by the policies created by the government case, but actually spooling the tale from completely different thread. The rationale of the opposition should be compelling as its own story and should regard the listeners as a biased audience (having just heard the government narrative). It is imperative that the story begins from the neutral setting and be built up from behind that perspective.

SPEAKER ROLES

The Leader of Opposition

The Leader of Opposition is the first to speak from the Opposition side of the House and the second to speak following the Prime Minister. The Leader of Opposition should clarify any *definitional* problems, *rebut* the Prime Minister's arguments, *outline* the Opening Opposition team's case, and *develop positive matter* in support of its case. Its speech should set the tone of the opposition bench and provide the overarching opposition theme for the round.

In an ideal debate round, the definition coming from the Prime Minister would be clear enough to simply move on with the rest of the round. In most of these debates, the Leader of Opposition won't even bring up the definition and would move directly into her case. Formally, some debaters would simply state, "We accept the definition as provided by the Opening Government." Unfortunately, ideal rounds do not occur all the time.

It is every debater's and adjudicator's fervent hope that they never have to experience a round with a definitional challenge. The round becomes an elaborate display of semantics, rather than a legitimate debate on the issues. However, as stated earlier, there are grounds for definitional challenges outlined by the WUDC Rules. The simple litmus test would always be, "Can we have a fair debate round given the definition of the Opening Government?" This is *not* the same thing as, "Does this make our job harder?"

Creating smoother ground for the opposition's position does not qualify for a reason to offer changes to or even challenge the definition. Clarifying the definition should only be left for verification and delineation of the forwarded philosophies or themes drawn out by the Opening Government. This should be left to points of information offered during the Prime Minister's speech rather than wasted on during the Leader of Opposition's speech.

Beyond this point, if the definition is clearly abusive, the only person in the round permitted to offer the definitional challenge is the Leader of Opposition. She must formally declare from the start of her speech, "We are challenging the definition as provided by the Opening Government." Then, she must announce which one of the definitional rules has been violated and briefly explain why it is a violation. Next, she should provide the definition as it should have been. Finally, she should set up her case as if the challenged definition never existed.

Definitions aside, the first real job that a Leader of Opposition must do is assess how much damage had been done by the Prime Minister. Here is where some debaters differ. Most debaters begin their speech with a rebuttal of the Prime Minister's speech. However, most Canadian debaters and those who typically get carried away with rebuttal prefer to save this for the last two minutes of their speech. The advantage of doing rebuttal from the top is getting a chance to deal with the holes of the government arguments as they are still fresh in both the minds of the speaker as well as the audience. The advantage of waiting for the end of the speech before providing rebuttal is that it provides better time management, lest the positive matter be rushed through. There are no advantages in terms of adjudication, as long as the speakers are clear with what they are doing and clarify this with signposting.

Rebuttal, as discussed with the role of the Deputy Prime Minister, is the response offered to the arguments forwarded by the side opposite. The Leader of Opposition's rebuttal is extremely significant since it is the first crack that the opposition benches get at the government case. It is also advisable for the Leader of Opposition to engage with the thematic elements used to set up the Government case, rather than just the lines of argumentation.

Outlining the Opening Opposition case vis-à-vis the Opening Government's case requires subtle adjustments and careful presentation. There are times when adjudicators have unfairly misunderstood unique arguments that would stand as positive matter in a round simply because the Leader of Opposition buried the presentation under the avalanche of rebuttal material. There should be a clear distinction between these elements and the Leader of Opposition should be delicate with how they choose to proceed. Positive matter coming from the Opposition benches should stand independently from the Government case. In other words, it would work just as well as if the Leader of Opposition presented her positive material as if she were the Prime Minister with an antithetical motion.

The Deputy Leader of Opposition

The Deputy Leader of Opposition is the second person to speak from the Opposition side of the House and the fourth speaker overall in the round following the Deputy Prime Minister. It is the Deputy Leader of Opposition's role to *rebut* the arguments of the Deputy Prime Minister and *develop positive matter* in support of the Opposition case, as promised by the Leader of Opposition.

Much like the Deputy Prime Minister, the Deputy Leader of Opposition has the unique ability to try to beat the closing teams to the punch. He has to decide which arguments are essential to the team's victory and which can be sacrificed, leaving them for the closing team to develop. This is potentially dangerous. If the Deputy doesn't "shut the door" on the most critical elements from his side of the House, the closing teams would exploit them and seem to do a much better job from that side of the House.

There are two schools of thought that prevail here. The first is deciding to "burn turf" or "matter dump." This is when the deputies try to cover as much ground as quickly as possible in the hopes that all the probable lines of argumentation that the closing team could extend would be exhausted. The practice is meant to erode as many ideas as possible so that the closing team would be shut out of the round without fertile ground to root its ideas, lest the credit for the arguments go to the opening team that first introduced the idea.

However, it isn't enough to simply mention the argument in order to lay claim to it. The second approach is far more effective and sensible. A debater must be able to develop the idea fully and provide the impact points to establish credibility. Without this, adjudicators would do little by way of recognition and simply think that the burned turf was chockfull of lines underdeveloped by the opening teams. This would render the half-baked ideas open game for the closing teams to develop fully and actually take full credit for. In a close debate rounds with good teams, burning turf isn't really a sound option at all.

This is why the deputy's job is sensitive and requires a lot of in-round decision making and strategy. It is ideal to work out the plan of attack and decide which arguments to leave on the table for the closing team during preparation time, but it will most likely have to be acted upon in the middle of the round. A good Deputy will always endeavor to make his teammates' points survive the onslaught of refutation that comes from the side opposite. He should also ensure that whatever promises were made by his partner (i.e., her split/her part of the case) should be kept before the end of his speech. Organization will obviously play a great part here, as there are several things to accomplish within the speech, so prioritization should always be a key.

REJECTING COUNTER PLANS AND COUNTER MODELS

Some teams decide to run *counter plans* or *counter models* from the Opening Opposition. This is something that is antithetical to any opposition philosophy and should *never* be used. A counter plan a case provided by an Opposition team that concedes the entire philosophy or theme of the government, but offers an alternative solution rather than the policy advocated. This might seem to be a fair compromise to the debate, but it results in virtually ending the debate.

Given the motion, "This House supports Capital Punishment," it would be totally unacceptable for a Leader of Opposition to say, "We agree with the Prime Minister's view on the dangers of a relaxed criminal justice system. We also agree that the death penalty is justified in certain cases. We just think that there should be tighter restrictions on the appeals system." This totally undermines the natural opposition principle against the use of capital punishment. A counter plan does not actually oppose the ideals, principles, or justifications forwarded by the side opposite. This is a lazy, disjointed, and academically dishonest way of confusing everyone in the round, trying to play both sides of the fence. Ironically, this format should never logically support such a strategy since the closing teams from the same side of the House would serve that very purpose. It may be true that there are teams that may have been successful from time to time using this tactic. This only comes from it becoming a very muddled round and by them out-confusing everyone else. But it never makes it right and it isn't good debating.

CHAPTER 7

The Closing Government

The third of the four teams in a debate round is called the **Closing Government**. It is comprised of two speakers, the Member of Government and the Government Whip. The function of the Closing Government team is to extend a clearly articulated case that upholds its side of the motion and refutes the case provided by the Opposition. Within the allotted 15-minute preparation time, only the two members of the team are permitted to work with each other. Building a Closing Government case consists of *developing an extension* and then *fulfilling the individual speaker roles* accordingly.

The closing teams are what make the WUDC format unique from any other in the world. The four-team format was developed to simulate the parliamentary reality of having multiple parties that may be on the same side of particular issues, but have varying perspectives on how the philosophies are best to be supported. This helps make the round a lot more interesting and digs the discussion of the issues as deep as it could possibly go. At an intervarsity debating tournament, it is most likely that the teams sharing the bench from one side of the House will not be from the same institution. Whether this is the case or not, closing teams are restricted to utilizing the preparation time only with their partner.

THE CLOSING GOVERNMENT EXTENSION

The 15-minute preparation time is an interesting period of both closing teams in the round. They are given the distinctive task of developing ideas for their side of the House knowing full well that the teams that precede them in the round might actually cover those precise issues. This doesn't mean that they should simply toss the issues and assume the worst. Preparing for the closing half of the round also doesn't consist of throwing caution to the wind and riding the coattails of the opening team. The preparation time should consist of compiling an intense collage of all the possible angles from that side of the House, then patiently observing throughout the first half of the round which ideas are developed fully by the opening team. This gives the closing team the opportunity to present the discarded, underdeveloped, and abandoned points as its extension.

There is one basic restriction on extensions. They must never be contradictory to the opening team's case. This means that the opening teams' philosophies and themes must be respected by the closing teams, and their material and models must still be able to work with whatever variants are offered by the extension. A contradiction between the opening and the closing teams is referred to as a "knife" as in a "knife in the back" as there is nothing more deplorable than that kind of betrayal.

The *only* exception to this is if there is a *definitional challenge* offered by the Leader of Opposition. If the Opening Government's definition is challenged be the Opening Opposition, then it is up to the Closing Government to choose one of three options. First, it may recognize the challenge as legitimate and accept the Opening Opposition's revised definition. Second, it can reject the challenge and support the original definition as provided by the Opening Government. Finally, it can accept the challenge, but if it finds that the Opening Opposition's revised definition is equally a violation of the rules, it may also challenge that definition and offer the third definition in the round. None of these options would be reflective of a good first-half debate, but the Closing Government at least has the potential of cleaning up the morass and thus saving the round from being a complete waste of time.

SPEAKER ROLES

The Member of Government

The Member of Government is the third person to speak from the Government side of the House and the fifth speaker overall in the round following the Deputy Leader of Opposition. It is the Member of Government's role to *extend* the team's case, including her new lines of argument, *rebut* the arguments of the Deputy Leader of Opposition, and *develop positive matter* in support of her case.

When the Member of Government presents her extension, it should be clearly delineated from the Opening Government's case. There should be no confusion as to where the Opening Government's case ends and where the Closing Government's case begins. Signposting is crucial to getting the ideas laid out specifically to the teams to which they belong. Making this distinction is the difference between letting the adjudicators know what the extension is and completely confusing them.

The Member of Government should keep in mind that she is supportive of the views forwarded by the Opening Government, but wants to do more than just a better job of presenting them. The ideas can be broader or more specific, depending on the strategy employed by the opening team. With the motion, "This House supports terrorism" and the Opening Government's case, which states, "We believe that the act of terrorism is justified, since oppressive governments merely tag legitimate freedom fighters as terrorists. They leave them little choice. We support the right for these citizens to rise up and fight for their freedoms, using violence if necessary."

Now if the entire Opening Government case is narrowed to the theme of "One man's terrorist is another man's freedom fighter" and the benefits that terrorism have had in many nations, then it would be possible for the Closing Government to extend the principle by saying, "We agree with our colleagues from the Government benches. Yes, there are oppressive governments and the benefits so these drastic actions have been well established by the Opening Government. We on Closing Government wish to extend this debate by looking at the external actors in these circumstances. We believe that it isn't right for other nations to engage in a War on Terror, and we demand that all international forces cease their patronage of oppressive governments across the globe."

Such an extension both supports the principles laid out by the Opening Government and provides an ample method by which Closing Government can find a unique perspective from which to debate. This broadens the scope of the round to discuss the value of external force that other nations exert from a "War on Terror." It becomes an additional talking point, but more important, it potentially can take a lot of the fire out of the Opening Government case and make the extension seem "more encompassing" by the end of the debate.

The rebuttal lines that the Member of Government draws during his speech should respond to the fundamental elements that still make the Opening Opposition relevant in the round. If the either or both the Deputy Prime Minister and the Deputy Leader of Opposition chose to burn turf during their speeches, the easiest mistake that the Member of Government can make would be to try to respond to everything left on the floor. Instead, he should carefully package all of the arguments currently on the floor into general themes and simplify the position of both opening teams using these themes. The Member would then use the themes of the Opening Government to introduce his extension and rebut the themes of the Opening Opposition. This way, he won't get bogged down by the intricacies that both teams just finished spending half the debate on already. This gives him the clear path to present his positive matter through the extension. The ideas are easier to now package as unique to the Closing Government and not thrown haphazardly with rebuttal material.

The Government Whip

The Government Whip is the fourth person to speak from the Government side of the House and the seventh speaker overall in the round following the Member of Opposition. It is the Government Whip's role to *rebut* the arguments of the Member of Opposition, and she *summarizes* the Closing Government's case and the debate as a whole. She *may* additionally develop new positive matter in support of her case if she so chooses, but with a few risks.

As the final speaker from the government benches, the Whip is given the difficult task of being the only person from that side of the House with the opportunity to respond to the Closing Opposition's extension. Several rounds have been lost by Government Whip speakers solely because they failed to address the extension case from the Member of Opposition. The reason why this is prospectively so damaging is that it gives the Closing Opposition a free pass and that case gets away unscathed.

Summarizing the debate is often the most misunderstood and misinterpreted role of any speaker in the entire debate. Many people have quickly confused this as a recounting of the debate, speaker-by-speaker and argument-by-argument. Although such a method is acceptable as a sufficient summary, the best method of summary is using the thematic approach. The Whip speaker could take a little time to categorize all of the points that come from both speakers from each team and condense them into the overarching themes that are either presented by the respective teams, or created by the Whip speaker themselves. This is a much more organized and easier method to digest the great depth of information that the round contained to this point.

So, it is unnecessary for the Whip to summarize each individual speech and refer to each individual speaker, as long as the most important elements that each team addressed in the round are attended to accordingly. The narrative is a powerful means of bringing the round's "story" to its eventual conclusion. Summarizing the round using a strong narrative can be incredibly persuasive and draw the adjudicators in with great interest.

The final role of a Government Whip is permitted by the rules, but remains completely optional. The Whip is allowed to introduce the last new lines of argumentation to the round. This option has the potential for great rewards, but it does come with a considerable risk. New lines of argumentation are an advantage for Closing Government teams with an incredibly large amount of material for their extension. The concept is quite simple: If the Member of Government can't get to it during her speech, then leave it to the Government Whip to clean up.

Unfortunately, it isn't cut and dried for the Closing Government. If it chooses to take this option, then it provides permission for the Opposition Whip to respond to the new material with new lines of refutation. A competent Opposition Whip would easily be able to utilize this opportunity to get the last say in the matter, and the Government would have no speech left to redirect the material back to its side.

CHAPTER 8

The Closing Opposition

The last of the four teams in a debate round is called the *Closing Opposition*. It is comprised of two speakers, the Member of Opposition and the Opposition Whip. The function of the Closing Opposition team is to extend a clearly articulated case that upholds its side of the motion and refutes the case provided by the Government. Within the allotted 15-minute preparation time, only the two members of the team are permitted to work with each other. Building a Closing Opposition case consists of *developing an extension* and then *fulfilling the individual speaker roles* accordingly.

THE CLOSING OPPOSITION EXTENSION

Some debaters think (incorrectly) that the closing opposition is the easiest position with which to use the 15-minute preparation time. It would seem as if they could sit through most of the debate, sifting through the ideas for the best arguments, then use them for the extension. This is plausible, but it does not consistently work to create a dynamic case. The extension coming from the Closing Opposition is the final salvo in the debate and should not be a simple rehash of what has been covered to this point. Instead, it should illustrate a fresh perspective with a unique opposition position on the round. The ideas must again be sensitive to the philosophies and themes drawn up by the Opening Opposition, and thereby find consistency. It is also not permitted for a Closing Opposition team to be inconsistent or knife the Opening Opposition.

Once more, the only circumstance when a closing team is permitted to knife its opening team is in the case of definitional challenges. There is only one possibility with which a Closing Opposition would face dealing with definitions at this late point in the round; under the horrid situation of having three definitions that violated the rules in the same round. If the Leader of Opposition and the Member of Government both challenged the definitions that came before them, the Member of Opposition can either accept one of the three definitions, challenge the Member of Government's definition, or provide a fourth definition. As odd and perverse as this circumstance might seem, this type of round has occurred in the past, much to the chagrin and frustration of those who were utterly unfortunate to witness it.

SPEAKER ROLES

The Member of Opposition

The Member of Opposition is the third person to speak from the Opposition side of the House and the sixth speaker overall in the round following the Member of Government. It is the Member of Opposition's role to *extend* the team's case including their new lines of argument, *rebut* the arguments of the Member of Government, and *develop positive matter* in support of his or her case.

This is the last chance for the Opposition to introduce new concepts to the round as it has been progressing. There are some Members of Opposition who neglect to get the new material in the round or worse, fail to label the extension as they introduce it. It is vital for them to clearly adopt the extension to the round before the end of their speech. There have been many adjudicators who have punished closing teams for their lack of distinctive contribution in a debate round. Even if the teams choose to develop points that were left raw by the Opening Opposition, the Member must be clear about this new spin and complete development of the initial ideas.

The Member of Opposition also has the duty of constructing the initial refutation of the Closing Government's extension. The rebuttal must address the exclusive points raised by the Member of Government, and not just serve as a whitewash of the entire government side of the House. The lines of refutation can be furthered later by the Opposition Whip, but they must be at the very least introduced before the end of the Member of Opposition's speech.

Since this speech will mark the last opportunity for the Opposition benches to introduce new material to the debate, the positive matter must be organized and developed completely. Some teams prefer to squeak in some lines of argumentation to the Opposition Whip's speech through subtle lead-ins from the

Member of Opposition, but they are gambling a great deal. If the lead-in from the Member's speech is too subtle or inconclusive, any material that comes in afterwards during the Whip's speech may be classified as new. This would be a violation and the Closing Opposition would be penalized.

The Opposition Whip

The Opposition Whip is the fourth person to speak from the Opposition side of the House and the eighth and last speaker overall in the round following the Government Whip. It is the Opposition Whip's role to *rebut* the arguments of the Government Whip and *summarize* the Closing Opposition's case and the debate as a whole. The Opposition Whip may *never* develop positive matter in support of his or her case, but he or she is permitted to *provide refutation* to any new matter offered by the Government Whip.

The type of summary that an Opposition Whip uses should be similar to the thematic style suggested for the Government Whip. In fact, the only difference between the Whip speakers (aside from their positions in the debate, of course) would be the use of new material. This rule is also often misunderstood because some people have wrongfully thought that no new matter means that the speaker cannot discuss anything unless it was previously introduced in the round. This is only partially true. The Opposition Whip cannot introduce new lines of argumentation, but he can (and should) produce new examples that further illustrate the previously introduced ideas. He should also rebut the new analysis (if any) from the Government Whip. But ultimately, the Opposition Whip should choose his or her words well because they will be the last spoken in the debate.

PART II

CHAPTER 9

Manner

Worlds Rule 4.1.1 Manner is the presentation of the speech. It is the style and structure a member uses to further his or her case and persuade the audience.

The second criterion of assessing a speech is manner. The easiest way of understanding manner is by considering everything that is perceived about a speaker by the audience's using all five senses. Or, in other words, manner is the "physical manifestation" of a person's speech. When witnessing a speech, quite obviously the audience will utilize their auditory and visual abilities to a far greater degree than their tactile, olfactory, or gustatory facility. To better understand the principal approach to each of the senses, they have been divided into two categories. What is seen, felt, tasted, and smelled by an audience is covered by **Stage Mastery**. What people in the audience hear is captured by **Voice Projection** and **Modulation**.

STAGE MASTERY

Stage Mastery is the speaker's total command of the physical space provided for his or her presentation. But even before the speaker opens his or her mouth and fires off a single syllable, he or she has already made an impression on the audience.

Some audience members might be progressive and not judge a book by its cover, but unfortunately, most of the crowd will go with their first instinct.

On the technical side of this issue, there are a few terms that need to be clarified when referring to the "stage." The stage itself is the provided area for a speaker to make her presentation. Sometimes, this is on a slightly raised platform called a *dais*, or a major platform as one might expect at an auditorium, coliseum, or arena. Other times, it could be from a *pulpit*, or a raised stand intended specifically for a single speaker much like those found in churches, temples, or cathedrals. Most everyone erroneously refers to the *podium* as the stage fixture from which a person speaks. That is actually a *lectern*. The reason for the common misuse of the term is that the lectern usually rests atop the podium. The bottom line is that a lectern is something you speak from; a podium is something you stand on.

What You See Is What You Get

The most immediate concern that a speaker has is the visual perception that the audience has of him or her. How a person is dressed, how she moves, and the faces she make will inevitably create others' first impressions. Understanding how to control these variables is not an attempt to change your personality, nor is it all required necessarily achieving success as a speaker. However, it would serve you well to at the very least be aware of how you look and understand what conscious or subconscious effect it may be having on your audience.

Attire and Appearance. Deciding what to wear for any speaking engagement depends entirely upon the objective of the speaker, how appropriate the outfit is for the event, and quite obviously that it falls within the boundaries of social decency. This, of course, is dictated primarily by the societal norms that the audience itself is observing. In other words, a college student in Southern California may wear something to his summer classes that would be significantly out of place if he was going in for a job interview in a corporate office in Tokyo. The dynamics of culture and climate will help a person determine if what he or she is wearing is suitable.

The easiest rule to follow is this: Wear something that will not say more to the audience than you do. If what you are wearing is distracting in terms of design, color, fabric, or fit, the best idea would be to change it. At debating tournaments, most people assume that you must wear business attire the whole way through. Not so. It is appropriate for competitors to wear what they would to their own university classes through the preliminary rounds.

Then, during the elimination rounds, they would wear the more formal attire. At large tournaments like Worlds, the Finals would require national dress or black tie. This means that gowns and tuxedos are worn alongside kimonos, kilts, barongs, dashiki, and other international formalwear.

For those who have not experienced making presentations with formal attire, it is advisable to get some practice. Observing oneself in front of a mirror may feel strange, but at least you will have some idea of what your audience will be looking at. It will also help to know how the material feels and fits so that you would have a clear idea if and how certain gestures could cause wardrobe malfunctions.

General grooming and neatness might seem obvious here, but there are those who will insist on making fashion statements. Once again, if your appearance makes the statement more than you do, you failed as a speaker. The conversation you want to avoid among audience members as they are leaving is,

"Did you see that tattoo? And the piercings? Wicked!"

"Yeah, but did you realize what he said?"

"I dunno. I wasn't really listening. But he was so cool . . ."

Nonverbal Communication. A lot of information can be transmitted intentionally or unwittingly by a speaker through his or her movements. After viewing a video replay of their speeches, several students have remarked, "I didn't know that my face looks like that when I talk," or asked "Why do my hands move like that?" Once again, unless you have spent time actually watching yourself speak in a mirror or observed yourself on a video recording, there is no way that you will have a complete picture of what you look like when you speak. Your posture, facial expressions, hand gestures, body position, and gait can be used to maximize the message that you are conveying. Used improperly, it will only confuse or distract your audience. It is essential to understand which movements or gestures to avoid and which are appropriate to provide emphasis.

Worlds Rule 4.2.4 Hand gestures will generally assist a member to emphasise important arguments. Excessive hand movements may, however, be distracting and reduce the attentiveness of the audience to the arguments.

Even the slightest raise of an eyebrow or hand movement can throw off an idea and make one idea mean something else to the person perceiving it. The best recommendation is to keep your feet shoulder-width apart, hands clasped lightly on the lectern (if available) or in front with arms bent (if lectern is not available) so that the hands remain near the midsection of the torso. This might seem or feel awkward at first, but it allows for more directed and controlled gestures or use of hands.

You must avoid folding your arms (nonverbal for "I am being defensive"), placing your hands behind your back ("I've got something to hide"), or on your hips ("I don't agree with you in the most stubborn way possible"). General shifting of body position and posture is a clear display of uneasiness and lets the audience in on your general lack of confidence and anxiety. Eye contact should be made as often as possible, but overcoming the natural fear that stems from doing so comes with practice. At the very least, try looking at the foreheads of your audience. This way, you give them the illusion that you are looking at them, but you don't have to lock-on with their "judgmental gaze."

Can You Feel It?

The tactile sense may not seem to be of great concern when preparing to speak. Although the speaker may (and should) not spend much time actually touching the audience members (and vice versa), the sense of touch still has a significant role.

Proximity.   The distance that a speaker has in relation to his or her audience is important because it is a source of comfort and meaning. This is usually first determined by the stage provided for the presentation. In a small room setting (i.e., classrooms, offices, or boardrooms), the presenter typically stands as listeners remain seated at a relative distance. Sometimes, presenters are provided a dais, but more often than not, they are expected to speak at the area provided right in front of their own seat. Classroom set-ups are a lot easier to manage since the front of the class always serves as the stage.

Some speakers like to casually walk closer to their audience. This is where proximity is of great consequence. If a speaker stands too close to the listeners, both will feel uncomfortable. If the speaker lingers at the back of the stage, the audience would perceive him to be fearful. Generally speaking, coming out from behind the lectern, or descending from the dais, stage, or pulpit gives the audience the sense that the speaker is being more personable. This technique can and should only be used at critical moments of a speech, usually during speeches that require empathy. This is often used by attorneys when they are trying to reach for the jury's heartstrings. Approaching an audience may also be used to intimidate them as well. Just don't overdo it.

Climate.   If it gets to be too cold or too hot on stage, speakers would not only find themselves distracted, but they will end up making their audience feel uncomfortable as well. For example, if it was too cold, the speaker might end up folding her arms or putting her hands in her pockets for relief. This would then send the wrong nonverbal signal and affect the presentation. It would also help to know if your attire makes you excessively warm and causes you to sweat. Profuse sweating can be a major distraction and will only make you feel that much more uncomfortable. Knowing how relax and cool down in an outfit will also be critical.

A Matter of Taste (and Smell)

If the gustatory and olfactory senses seem to have even less to do with speaking than the tactile sense, that's because they do. There are, however, a few simple ideas to remember. First, always remember to hydrate yourself properly. It is recommended to always have easy access to a glass/bottle/container of water available throughout any speaking engagement. Carbonated sodas or sports drinks are not advised as they will not help the vocal cord lubrication process and actually cause more discomfort.

Gum or candy (or any other food for that matter) should never be consumed at any time during a presentation. Not only is it considered highly uncouth and inappropriate, but it is also very distracting. The ability to consistently enunciate words is tremendously jeopardized. Many people assume that it is acceptable to chew gum while speaking to overcome anxiety, but this is quite simply making the matter a whole lot worse. The last image that you want to project of yourself to your audience is you among a herd of cattle masticating the juicy cud.

The sense of smell is often assaulted by speakers unfamiliar with the notion that too much of a good thing is bad for you. They are quite liberal with their application of colognes, perfumes, bug sprays, deodorants, or other assorted atomizers that render the audience with the awful sensation of entering a *cougar* convention. The dizzying and oft-time nauseating effect on your listeners with this mass of odors could be rather suffocating, and tragically, easily avoided. However, the complete absence of any deodorant when it is actually necessary is even more tragic.

Can You Hear Me Now?

The sense of hearing is easily the most essential when assessing a speech. The ability to discern audio nuances during a speech can make the difference between *hearing* what is being said and actually *listening* to the message.

Worlds Rule 4.2.3 Voice modulation will generally assist a member to persuade an audience as the debater may emphasise important arguments and keep the attention of the audience. This includes the pitch, tone, and volume of the member's voice and the use of pauses.

VOICE PROJECTION

Many people assume that a loud booming voice is always the best bet. They think that a firebrand sermon hailed down from a preacher will win every debate. Or that the only effective speeches are those bellowed by pep rally leaders. Although those speakers can be valuable, speaking loudly is neither a guarantee nor a prerequisite for speech efficacy. Voice projection is the complete control of a speaker's volume. This means that is used correctly, a whisper could be even more powerful than a scream.

The first component of volume control involves the *speech pattern rate*. The intensity of a person's voice shouldn't originate from their vocal cords. It actually should start from the diaphragm. The speaker should learn how to breathe in deeply through the nose, and then channel the air that comes from the diaphragm in the exact way that singers practice. The actual volume is controlled by how fast the air travels through the vocal cords. So, ironically, if you wish to speak louder, you should actually slow the rate of your speech. People instinctively speak faster and more excitedly. True, they will be loud. But over time, they will strain their vocal cords. Additionally, the quality of their voice is extremely diminished. If a person speaks at such a rapid pace, he loses control of their volume and rarely even knows whether his voice is heard or understood. The words are often distorted, and the speaker will end up with a confused audience and a sore throat.

The second component is *focus*. The desired target for a speaker should always be the members of the audience furthest away. These are usually the people seated at the back of the room. Speakers should use different levels in their volume and practice given that specific room's acoustics. If possible, I highly suggest that a speaker visit the speaking venue with a friend long before the engagement. Here, she can safely practice and find dead spots and echo zones with her naked voice. Having a friend help sort through the different levels as he or she sits in the area farthest from you will allow you to create a volume plan for the room. It is also advised that you conduct a conversation with the friend from the far reaches of the room.

Practice is especially important when speaking with a microphone. There is nothing worse than a hearing a person who yells into a microphone as if he didn't have one. Through time and much experience, a speaker will be able to master his volume enough to immediately know which levels to use in a room he's never even set foot in before.

Volume should be controlled relative to the appropriate triggers in a speech. It may crescendo right at the most impactful part of the speech, but a quiet voice can also be effective. The *pin-drop* technique is when a speaker gradually builds her volume up to a loud climax. Then, after she waits a few moments (letting everyone hang in silence enough to hear a pin-drop), she whispers the most crucial line in the presentation. This might seem overly dramatic for some, but it is very effective. This technique is often used by lawyers and barristers in courtrooms.

Being able to manipulate your voice using subtle changes in your volume can help you achieve high stages of persuasion. But the most important factor with voice projection is that you remain audible and intelligible. Nobody likes being yelled at all the time. Nor do people particularly enjoy listening to a speaker who seems to have the mute button perpetually pushed. Balance and control should always be the goal.

VOICE MODULATION

Voice modulation is the pitch, intonation, and overall sound quality of a speaker's voice. The objective of every speaker should always be to learn how to provide color, light, and shade to his or her voice when speaking. Some people assume that inflecting your voice should only be preserved for actors, comedians, or any other stage performer. Actually, everyone should have emotional direction in the voice at all times. If not, he or she will suffer the consequence of having just one tone—thus becoming monotonous.

This doesn't mean that everyone should engage extreme tonal changes with even the briefest exchanges. But there is absolutely nothing wrong with adding a hint of emotion to brighten someone's day and to seem a little more than an android. Now, given a larger amount of time with a fixed audience, you can imagine how much more spirit is required to grab the audience's attention and present a meaningful message. The difficulty here is finding the balance. Speaking effectively will not require one to adapt his or her voice with the tonal qualities of a radio disc jockey or professional voice actor. But being able to accurately stimulate emotions from your audience is a desired skill. Aside from having the ability to evoke emotions through vocal tones, there are three other voice modulation aspects that a speaker must consider. These are enunciation, pronunciation and accent.

Enunciation is the intelligibility of the sounds formed by the speaker. A speaker is successful if the words come out clearly with discernable syllables. A person with poor enunciation would typically sound like he has a lisp or mutters his words incomprehensibly. People who mumble or create sounds that slur into each other often have issues with speaking too quickly. Another issue is that people rarely exercise their facial muscles before they speak. They usually get by each day by speaking without fully forming their words as they speak. Now, overexaggerating the facial movements while you speak looks, well, weird. There is no need to replicate the way that John Mayer looks like when he performs. As previously suggested, practicing in front of a mirror to know exactly what you look like will help.

Pronunciation differs from enunciation in that it deals with the way the words are designed to sound with the given language. This includes knowing when and how to use stress patterns with the syllables of each word. Obviously, this is usually learned through a lifetime of language use and experience, but checking the dictionary for the proper pronunciation of a word is your best bet. The reason why this is more important in modern society is that many words are improperly pronounced by so many people that it becomes "acceptable" by a lazy few and requires so little to perpetuate the linguistic abomination. Then, when faced with a formal presentation, the speaker has not acquired the discipline to pronounce the word correctly and simply sounds uneducated. Learning how words are supposed to be pronounced may seem basic, but it should never be taken for granted.

There is, however, an important distinction to be made. *Accent* affects pronunciation in a very significant way, but unless it is completely unintelligible, it should not be faked or arbitrarily changed. Regional, cultural, and multilingual experience will shape the accent that a speaker utilizes. But, since there is no "one" exact accent for a multicultural language like English, the learning curve when faced with multiple accents may be extremely steep. Consistency with the accent is what will help determine "proper" pronunciation in these cases.

For example, an Aussie might "sigh a few words in a different why" rather than "say a few words in a different way" from a Scottish, Irish, Chinese, Jamaican, or American speaker. But since he has been consistently using the same accent with the entirety of his lexicon, following what he is saying will just take some exposure and a lot of listening practice.

The difference also has a lot to do with vocal cadence. For example, having a questioning intonation at the end of a sentence is obviously used to ask questions. But with many Americans and Australians, "uptalking" is used even for declamatory statements. This will leave the audience with the feeling that the speaker is unsure of himself. Sadly, since this has become so much a part of how the speaker has learned and used his language, he is scarcely aware of it and probably doesn't even know when he are doing it or that it's even an issue.

Once more, I am not suggesting that people change their accents. The worst thing ever for a speaker to do is put on a faux accent. There is nothing more embarrassing than to watch someone "try" an accent while a specific audience winces at the attempt. But I do think that there is clearer way of speaking without laying the accent on thick. In other words, if a speaker is aware that she may be misunderstood by an audience, she could try to balance out her accent by emphasizing enunciation and pronunciation. If she can't eliminate accent issues, at least she can help neutralize the gap as much as possible.

CHAPTER 10

Achieving Clarity

Diction is a term often considered solely as a synonym to enunciation. Actually, this is the secondary meaning of the word. Diction actually refers to word choice in a given context. The richness of language gives the speaker a near infinite amount of word combinations with which to present ideas. This must come with three caveats that will help determine the desired effect on an audience. Words must be used with *accuracy*; the speaker must explain or avoid *jargon*; and *colloquialism* should be extremely limited or if possible, even eliminated.

Worlds Rule 4.2.5 Language should be clear and simple. Members who use language which is too verbose or confusing may detract from the argument if they lose the attention of the audience.

Accuracy with word use is essential when trying to relate a precise idea to the listener. There are many times when speakers can be quite careless with the words that they use and mismanage the message they mean to convey. Other times, there are speakers who are a little too liberal with their use of absolutes. "People will *always* benefit from this policy," or "*Everybody* understands why we need this change." At first, this might seem a bit nitpicky, but in the end, it may simply discredit the speaker for her overuse of hyperbole.

Vague language should never (and I really do mean *never* in this instance) be used. The favorite word of all vague speakers is "they." "*They* will get upset," or "This will only hurt *them* in the end." When you are discussing a person running an organization that affects a community and another company, knowing who he or she is without clarification would be disastrous. It is integral to engage with your audience as much specification as possible. The overuse of "we" is equally disturbing, especially since the audience does not know on whose behalf the speaker is speaking. This is especially evident when listening to an American debater addressing an international audience who continues to substitute the United States and/or its government with "we" or "us."

Ambiguity is also found in speakers' inclination to use key words repetitively in their speech. They fall in love with the word or phrase and then continually use it even out of logical or grammatical context. This also usually happens with catch phrases or idiomatic expressions, which can lead to some comical malapropisms or spoonerisms that unfortunately come at the speaker's expense. If the speaker focused on using simpler language without trying to impress the audience with his vocabulary (or lack thereof) or clever (so they thought) wordplay, then the message would be that much clearer.

Simplicity doesn't always mean simplistic. The listener is not going to be impressed by how many eight-syllable words you are able to use. The audience won't be any more persuaded by your mastery of the thesaurus or dictionary. Ultimately, if they don't know what a word means, your audience might simply turn to the person seated next to them and say, "Wow, this speaker is really good. But what does pneumonoultramicroscopicsilicovolcanoconiosis mean?" While this little conversation is going on (as with all the others in the audience as well), you have successfully distracted everybody from the main point. The audience might even remember the word more than the speech itself, which is never the goal. You could have simply said "severe lung disease" and spared yourself the self-inflicted interruption.

Jargon refers to context-specific language that requires previous experience with the subject matter or prior usage. This language alienates the audience members who are not experts in the field covered by the speaker's subject matter. This also includes the use of acronyms and shortcut language popularized by text and instant messaging. As much as possible, jargon should be avoided. If this is not at all possible, the speaker needs to spend some time explaining the meaning of the word or phrase or at least the context in which it is being used. Not doing so might leave the audience feeling like they walked into an inside joke that only the speaker was privy to. This doesn't mean that you have to go to the other extreme either. "You like the ocean, right? Have you ever gone Self Contained Underwater Breathing Apparatus diving before?" is just plain silly. Knowing what the audience can pick up through the context clues you provide will help a great deal as well.

There are debating terms that are considered jargon as well. This "debate-speak" seems useful when trying to maximize the allotted time for your speech, but it should never get in the way of an effective speech. Sometimes the terms are equally insufficient in conveying a persuasive argument. An example of this is the term "turn." The rationale for using the term is to imply that you are "turning" the arguments raised by the side opposite against them. Unfortunately, some debaters think by simply saying the word, the job is automatically done for them. There are no magic words, there are no pass codes. The measure of a brilliant speech isn't found by counting how many buzzwords are used, but the fashion by which they were utilized.

Using colloquialisms in a formal speech is like wearing denim shorts and an "I'm with Stupid" t-shirt to the prom. You might get away with it, but is it really worth it? People think that if you use hip lingo, slang, or coarse language, you will sound "real." Using expletives and other forms of questionable language will only make you vulgar and crude. You are not going to win an audience by somehow proving to them that you have "street cred."

You should also be wary of using regionally accepted idiomatic expressions. "What a complete furphy! I thought the bangarang had done them up like a kipper. But they were just taking the mickey out of us." Slang expressions are colorful and could be enjoyed as witty metaphors. At times, they could even be useful and help persuade the audience. This is only if they are familiar with the terms that the speaker is using. If not, it could just be a lot of jibber jabber.

Ultimately, clarity is achieved with accurate, simple, and universal language that any audience can comprehend.

CHAPTER 11

Entertaining the Audience

The only thing more daunting than trying to make an audience laugh is trying to instruct someone how to exactly make it happen. Thankfully, this is not the objective of this chapter. It should be noted, however, that humor plays a significant role in making the speech both engaging and memorable. Additionally, using analogies, relevant anecdotes, and witticisms may help the audience connect the necessary dots and understand the message fully.

There are speeches that focus on being *informative*, those that are intended to *persuade*, and those given deliberately to *entertain*. Although, the objective of those speeches is meant to lean toward a specific characteristic, each of these elements should be present in any speech. Usually speakers abandon one or even two of the other elements from their speeches. Some speakers rely too much on inundating their audience under a tsunami of information; others hide behind rhetorical wordplay and logical loopholes; and some basically try running a standup comedy routine. But it is important for *all* speeches to provide information in a persuasive and entertaining way. Finding the balance is quite tricky and is often lost to even the most experienced speakers.

Usually, the first element to be forsaken is the ability to entertain. After all, debates are about persuasion and information. But unless the audience is interested in the information and engaged enough to be persuaded, the opportunity to connect with them in the most memorable way could be easily squandered.

Listening to a public speaker is a lot like meeting a blind date. You both want it to go well and have the highest hopes for a successful encounter. With high anticipation and mounting pressure, nerves often seem a bit more frayed from the outset. This tension continues until someone makes the first move to break it. So, during the date, he tells a joke. If funny, the date would think, "Hmm, this person just made me laugh. Maybe this night will be great after all." If not so funny, she will start searching for the excuse to end the date right there.

Humor is used by many speakers as the way to break the ice with an audience. But it is a gamble. The first step is to determine whether you are naturally funny. This should be easy enough. If you often find things funny that no one else seems to laugh at or tell jokes to people who politely chuckle or maintain quizzical or stoic faces at the punch line, you are not funny. This doesn't mean that you should give up here and now. The problem is actually in your delivery.

Learning how to be animated during the set-up, but not overly so, then maintain a deadpan face at the punch line and have the right comic timing to pull it off takes a lot of practice. Sure, there are those who are naturally funny and seem to get this right away, but others actually have to hone the skill. Even the top comedians in history have run into cold audiences or bad patches in their routines. They too, have to practice.

Now, *finding* humor isn't the same as *forcing* it. You shouldn't try to be funny just for the sake of it. This will lead to you saying things you actually didn't mean to say. These comments will undoubtedly sound awkward and may even be interpreted to be politically incorrect or outright offensive. You will soon discover that there is no recovery from saying something to get a rise out of the crowd and having it backfire. It should be fairly obvious, but statements that tightrope across racist, sexist, or other insulting borders should be discarded.

There are some people who take this to the opposite extreme and are far too sensitive about everything. This is an important feature when strategizing the best way to present your ideas and when and what to allow yourself some leeway with. For example, making jokes that are "too soon" or tasteless because of the relative immediacy to a tragic event would never be the way to a crowd's heart.

This brings us to a sensitive area in this activity. Many years ago, there were several debate coaches throughout the Unites States who incorrectly generalized that all debaters in the WUDC format did was, "insult each other and tell jokes." The reputation was unwarranted. They were referring to occasional debates occurring among teams who were friends with each other and the adjudication panel. The debaters would rib and roast one another through the round as it progressed. As a few of these coaches were in attendance at such debates, they mistook this for a feature of the format. Truth be told, these *ad hominem* (or attacks made against the person rather than the arguments that they are making) are like cheap shots in sport. Just because a few people have done them, it should not be used to personify the whole event. Additionally, adjudicators are permitted to assess and penalize those who use personal attacks. The easiest rule to follow is not to do it. The payoff will never exceed the risk.

Knowing the proper context and when to be funny in a way that doesn't interrupt, corrupt, or confuse the message is essential. There might be times where the speaker is tempted to be careless with a comment, thinking that it would get a few laughs, but it isn't worth it if it comes at the expense of being an effective and credible speaker. Once more, humor shouldn't be the goal, but a tool to help achieve it.

Anecdotes, analogies, and general witticisms may be used in a speech as long as they are clearly and cleanly linked to the main idea and relevant to the overall message intended for the audience. These can be useful lenses that can aid the listeners when they do not fully understand what the point of the speaker is. Many ideas that are constructed for a debate stemmed from research and a lot of processing. An audience will not necessarily have the same amount of experience with the ideas as the speaker does or even be aware of the situational context from which the ideas come. Finding analogous ideas helps stimulate connections for the general principle that the speaker is presenting that might be lost on an uninformed audience. By using a well-formed analogy, the audience can follow the logical flow through a communal reference point. Incidentally, this chapter (as well as every other, for that matter) is chockfull of analogies if you have been paying attention.

This, however, can (and often does) lead to speakers' getting carried away with the analogy. They take the analogy too far where the link between the idea and what it was being analogized with starts to stretch thin and at times disappears completely. Another mistake is when they fall in love with the analogy and completely forget what it was being used to explain. Finally, there are those who didn't do a good job in thinking their analogy through and run into flaws in the analogy's logic. This is a huge problem since their opposition will gleefully take the analogy apart and the purpose for it is rendered useless.

If relevant humor is handled properly, the audience will respond like putty in a sculptor's hands. People love to laugh. They like hearing stories. If they can be entertained while they are being informed and persuaded, they will buy what the person is selling much more readily than from the robot from the opposition.

CHAPTER 12

Debate Etiquette

Like any other event or activity in the world, debating has its own set of customs, traditions, and decorum. Following these behavioral guidelines is expected from every debater, adjudicator, and audience member during any debate whether it's a simple practice debate or the World Grand Final. This chapter will discuss the conduct that is expected from anyone who participates in a debate round.

From the time that debaters and adjudicators gather together in the auditorium or briefing room, it should be fairly obvious that they are doing the same thing that everybody else is. They are sizing up their competition. The typical tournament will observe each team sitting cloistered together saying nothing more than, "Sorry this seat is taken," with halfhearted smiles for anyone else who approaches. There will be those who will claim that this is part of gamesmanship or that they are just nervous and trying to focus, but while you are waiting for announcements to be made? It may not sound like much, but some of the best friends you could ever make will come from this activity. It would be a shame if you didn't try to meet some of the most incredibly interesting people in the world when you have the chance. At the very least, don't be rude. You are just demonstrating your insecurities.

When any announcement is being made, however, it is common to see people stop talking or unplug from their iPods and ask, "Pairings?" then plug back in or return to the conversation immediately when they realize that the pairings aren't out yet. The worst part about this is that these are the same debaters and adjudicators who will claim that no announcement was made for this or that. The easiest thing in the world to do is to give your attention and obtain the information. This is not like the flight attendant telling you about the safety features of the aircraft. The very least you can do for all of the valuable effort that tournament organizers struggle with to make your experience more enjoyable is to listen to them and pay them the respect they deserve.

When the pairings go up, there is usually a mad rush to the front for those who cannot see. This is fine, but when people get the necessary information, they should permit others in the room the same opportunity. There are times when debaters (sometimes even adjudicators) will become disruptive as they are astonished, excited, or devastated by the match-up for the round. These dramatic displays are funny (maybe) the first time around, but extremely annoying when you are desperately trying to find your team name, position, opponents, and room as they crawl up the screen.

When the motion is released, please try to reserve your anguish until it's been read aloud. Most debaters are so keen on freaking out that they actually get the wording incorrect. This courtesy should extend, however, to those sitting around you. It is hard enough to ensure that you get the motion verbatim in the excitement and tension of the moment that it is released. It is that much harder with the inconsiderate groaning and screaming of people crowding nearby.

Finding the proper place to prepare your case can be challenging. It is customary to give the Opening Government team the room during prep time, and this should be strictly observed—that is, if you want to make sure you get a good definition. You should ensure that you are not in eavesdropping range from any other team. It would be wise to choose a place near the designated room for your round. This way, you don't get carried away with your prep time and have to run halfway around the campus searching desperately for the room if you go overtime. Being late for a debate round is not only poor form, it is actually dangerous. If you don't turn up in a time relatively close to the end of the 15-minute prep period, the organizers could activate a shadow team that could replace you at a moment's notice. If you are near the room, noticing all the people entering the room would be a great reminder that time is probably up.

Some IVs will require you to write your names on a white/blackboard, but typically this is not necessary since the ballot should have all the names properly listed on it. At other tournaments, the chair will pass the empty ballot around for you to fill in the team and speaker names. The Chair will usually ask each team what speaking order will be employed by each team before the round begins. Then he or she will call the House to order.

You might notice that people don't applaud the way they normally do at any other event. At a debate round, you will notice people tapping their hand on their lap or on a table. This is actually the proper way of applauding during a debate. The reason for this comes from the high-pitched sound of a clap. It actually drowns out the sound of anyone's voice. This is most noticeable during the President's State of the Union Address. You will notice that when Congress claps, the President has to remain silent until the audience quiets down. This isn't the case with a lower-toned tapping.

If a debater says something that many people really like, you might notice some people saying, "Hear, hear." This is the shortened version of "hear ye, hear him." This is an accepted compliment made of the person speaking. Conversely, you might hear the occasional "shame," the shortened version of "for shame," which is quite obvious if the audience vehemently disagrees with the point you are making. Neither of these should be abused, as it will never make an argument more convincing one way or another. It just gets progressively more irritating.

When a Chair calls for order, he really means it. Murmuring or talking while a debater is presenting her speech is incredibly disrespectful. Trying to whisper is also different from actually whispering. In this situation, the thought doesn't count. The idea of a whisper is that nobody should hear it other than your partner. Additionally, it is not acceptable for you to converse with other teams in the round or any audience member while the debate or verbal adjudication is ongoing.

All speakers should wait for the Chair to recognize them before they stand to speak. You may be really excited to speak and want to get geared up for it as quickly as possible, but you should really wait until you are given the floor before you take it. The permission to speak isn't just about etiquette, but it is also to ensure that the adjudicators aren't rushed with their note taking and the preparation they need before you take the floor. Getting up before you are called is a nonverbal for them to rush from you. Never a good thing.

Points of information. In terms of etiquette, this is probably the most abused, ignored, and generally disregarded element in a debate round. Proper decorum should be observed by both the person offering the point of information as well as the speaker granting them the floor.

Worlds Rule 1.4.2 To ask a Point of Information, a member should stand, place one hand on his or her head, and extend the other towards the member speaking. The member may announce that they would like to ask a "Point of Information" or use other words to this effect.

Debaters rarely put their hand on their head when they rise for a point of information these days. It was previously a requirement and part of tradition. The custom started with the old Parliament where the members used to wear wigs. When they would rise for a point of information excitedly, their wigs would fall off. Thus, began the practice of leaving your hand on your head. Now, debaters simply stand and extend their hand out palm facing upwards. However, it isn't strange and it's rather refreshing to see a debater offer a point of information in the old-school fashion once in a while.

It is, however, unacceptable for a debater to remain seated when he offers a Point of Information. The speaker, unless physically unable, must rise for a Point of Information. Additionally, it is no longer necessary to say anything when you stand to offer a point. The only reason why debaters used to say anything aloud was to get the attention of a speaker if his or her back was to them. But in most rounds, the opposing debaters are well within the vantage point of the speaker. This would mean that nothing need ever be said by the debater offering the point of information. This is for two reasons: It is unnecessarily disruptive, and it defeats the whole purpose of requiring the permission of the speaker. If the debate is held in a large auditorium or theater and the speaker's back is to the rest of the debaters (Set-up 3 in Chapter 2), then one would understand that getting the speaker's attention might require the person offering the point of information to actually say, "On that point," or "Point of Information." This, however will simply not do in a smaller room with much more sensitive acoustics. With potentially four people yelling variations of "On that point!" it is impossible for the adjudicators to accurately hear what the speaker is saying. Once again, if the speaker can see you, just stand up.

Second, it is an abusive practice to say things like "On Rwanda" or "On the civil disobedience practices in India." This is a cheap shot to get your point across without having the permission from the speaker who has the floor. It is tantamount to offering a Point of Information anyway. This is not only rude, it is tremendously bad form. Sportsmanship is far more important that gamesmanship. If you try to do this, adjudicators should (and will) punish you.

Worlds Rule 1.4.3 The member who is speaking may accept or decline to answer the Point of Information.

The person speaking controls the floor. This means that she has the right to decline the Point of Information by politely asking the person to be seated. Traditionally, the speaker would say something like, "No thank you, please take a seat" or "Not at this time." This was simplified by a hand gesture, slowly waving down the debaters offering the points of information. This was first popularized by Ben Richards at the 1994 Worlds Semifinals. When he first did the gesture, none of the debaters who were offering the Points of Information knew what was going on until Ben said, "*This* means sit."

The speaker should always be clear if she is indeed granting permission to the debater offering by saying something like "Your point, please." If a speaker sees someone offering a Point of Information and knows that she is about to conclude the point she is currently making but wishes to grant them the time soon afterwards, she may say, "I'll take you in a moment." This will permit the debater to continue standing until the floor is yielded as promised.

When there is more than one person standing to offer a Point of Information, the speaker must always be clear about which person she is choosing. She should *never* say things like "You choose among yourselves" or "I'll take one of you." But when she picks the specific person, it isn't good form for the person chosen to turn to his partner and say, "You do it." A speaker should always take notice of people rising for a Point of Information and allow them the courtesy of being seated. Don't keep the debaters standing for minutes on end. Don't be lazy to make the simple gesture and let them know that you don't intend to take them at that particular time.

Remember, it is proper etiquette to allow two or three Points of Information during your speech. Don't take them back to back. You are not running a press conference. Prioritize the person you call based on who stood first or who has been more persistently sat down by you. It is also advisable to take one Point of Information from the opening team and one from the closing team. Never ask for Points of Information if they are not being offered.

Conversely, if you are seated by the speaker, you should not have a "spring attached to your seat" and stand right back up like a whack-a-mole. Give the speaker the courtesy of continuing a bit more when you are sat down. If there are others standing as you are and the speaker chooses one of the others, sit down immediately as the other person is granted the floor or if he or she is told that he or she will be taken in a moment. The speaker just took a Point of Information and will (should) not take one immediately after. Also, try to keep your grumbling about "not being the one being called" or about "being denied the Point of Information" to yourself. The more you audibly complain about not being called, the less likely you actually will be. Nobody likes a whiner.

Worlds Rule 1.4.4 Points of Information should not exceed 15 seconds in length.

When you are offered a Point of Information, don't spend a lot of time with jokes. Get to the point as quickly as possible. Some chairs or timekeepers will call out "15" to indicate that the time allotted has elapsed. But a person offering a Point of Information should never let it get to that point. If it does, chances are, the point is too long. The person offering a Point of Information should also sit down as soon as he is done offering the point. He relinquishes the floor as soon as the speaker starts responding to the point, regardless of how short the Point of Information was. In other words, Points of Information are not 15-second cross-examination periods. This is never a good strategy since the speaker and the adjudicators would probably only remember the first idea that you bring up during the 15 seconds you are allotted. It is far better to make your point short and concise.

Worlds Rule 1.4.5 The member who is speaking may ask the person offering the Point of Information to sit down when the offeror has had a reasonable opportunity to be heard and understood.

This is another abused rule in terms of etiquette. More often than not, speakers would allow the person to get in a couple of phrases during the Point of Information then rudely cut the person off before he or she could even get to the point. This results in both debaters trying to speak over the quickly rising voice of the other. I always felt it a better strategy to allow the person to complete the Point of Information and let the chair or timekeeper cut the person off by calling out "15." Instead of getting frustrated, I recommend concentrating on the response you intend to give for the first or most important part of it. That way, after your devastating response to the Point of Information, you leave the debater with the knowledge that he just wasted his time meandering on and on.

At the conclusion of the round, the chair will invite the teams to "cross the House." This means that teams should shake hands and congratulate each other for the debate. Then the chair will ask for the teams to vacate the room. Teams are expected to wait outside in the hallway for the verbal adjudication. Please note that while it is great to make friends and talk to your competitors and friends from other rounds that are also waiting for their respective results, adjudication panels are inside the rooms trying to reach their decision. So please try to keep it down. The deliberation process is difficult enough without a ruckus from outside.

Chairs and panelists should be respectful of each other, and they should never threaten or abuse one another. You should recognize that adjudicators disagree with one another just as often as debaters do. Amicable decisions may not always be reached, but at the very least, respect for each other should be maintained.

When the Chair calls all the teams back in for the result, he will generally first give the team ranking, provide the rationale for the decision, welcome comments from the other panelist, and then entertain general questions from the debaters. The panel may offer specific details and comments when they declare the round over and release the round, but that is up to the teams if they wish to approach them. This is *never* an opportunity to berate, attack, or insult any adjudicator. At no point should this ever be done. When all is said and done, proper debating etiquette is really about being fair and patient with others and observing the same kind of respect that you wish from others.

PART III

CHAPTER 13

Method

Worlds Rule 4.3.1 The elements of structure include the structure of the speech of the member and the structure of the speech of the team.

With morbid fascination, observe if you will a gaggle of teenage girls as they prattle on and on about, well, we're not quite sure. The non sequitur rambling of disjointed ideas and incoherent expression is basically watching a verbal train wreck. As entertaining as this stream of consciousness gabfest might be for a few moments, it ultimately is a complete waste of your time. It would have been far easier to understand them if they took the time to organize what they were articulating and each found the time to focus on a main point. Instead, we are witnesses to a chaotic blathering of undeveloped communication.

This brings us to the third and final criterion that we use to evaluate a speech. The logical progression of a person's speech is integral to comprehending his or her ideas and following the message. Method consists of how a speaker *organizes* the arguments, *analyzes* the evidence, and *synthesizes* it all into a point. This is often referred to as structure.

There are two types of method. The first is *internal method*, or the structure found in an individual's independent speech. The other is *external method*, which is the structure necessary for team consistency. Developing ways to achieve both will be discussed over the next two chapters. This chapter will focus on organization, analysis, and synthesis in a speech and understanding how it affects a debate round.

ORGANIZATION

The most important factor in organization is to understand what the objective of the speech is. This might sound obvious and rather intuitive, but the purpose of the speech is often the most neglected part. Losing sight of a speech's objective is typically at the heart of most disorganized speeches. This is tantamount to writing a thesis paper without a thesis. Without purpose, the speaker may wander off on tangents and lose her audience in the process. With a clear purpose, a speaker can craft her speech with far more control and direction. The crucial element here is to find balance between the speech and all the other dynamics of the debate surrounding it. Learning how to get back to the speech's objective after being interrupted by Points of Information, having to provide refutation, and keeping with the general themes of the round is rather challenging. This will be tackled in the next chapter.

Another significant factor of organization is for the speaker to know exactly where he is in the speech at all times. This is a lot more manageable when the speech is prepared, practiced, or even memorized long in advance. But with impromptu or extemporaneous speeches that have limited preparation time, this is not a luxury. In most cases, this will require the speaker to utilize notes.

If the speaker is using note cards, it advisable that the cards be no larger than 3" × 5". Most debaters use legal pads and have their notes scrawled out in various formats. This works fine, but the sort of notes brought up to the lectern has a direct correlation with the type of organization an audience can expect from the speech. The more disheveled the notes are on the page, the more likely the speaker will be flipping back and forth page after page, incredulously trying to decipher the mysterious glyphs and muttering audibly, "Why can't I read my own handwriting?"

The problem is that some speakers try desperately to infuse formulaic systems that allow them to simply plug in the changing values as they come. In other words, they create a paradigm to use for every speech and simply fill in the blanks when the motion is released. Somewhat like *Mad Libs* for debate. This was designed to make their lives easier, but will eventually make matters worse. Sure, the speech will have structure and will *seem* organized, but it will lack the depth of creativity and will miss the connection to the round itself. Organization is really about direction and control. The more discipline that a speaker practices in her speech, the less she needs to worry about getting lost in it.

ANALYSIS

By its very definition, analysis requires any matter to be taken apart and have each of its fragments evaluated separately. This helps people study even the most complex ideas, arguments, or other material in the process. This is typically required of paradigms so complicated that being able to break them apart simplifies the process and avoids the overwhelming nature that usually just confuses the examination.

Being able to analyze the materials used in speeches is critical to all debating. However, any straightforward observation of the analytical process necessary for a speech would only prove that it has to be done systematically. One procedure of approaching this is by using the same principles developed for *rhetorical criticism*. By applying certain measures developed for that discipline, debaters would be able to extract a lot more detail for the debate round than simply engaging in the more pedestrian approach. The more complex the idea, the more meticulous the debater has to become. This means that a debater must examine his or her very own process as much as he or she scrutinizes the material used in the round.

Rhetorical criticism is an excellent technique to help the debater analyze the matter used in a round in a clear and thorough way. The first step is to identify the rhetorical artifacts used in the round. Rhetorical artifacts are the model, evidence, and other data offered by both teams in their respective speeches. Rhetorical criticism requires the debater to use a filter while examining a specific artifact to help understand its place in the network or ideas. For example, in the debate round, "This House believes that a developing nation must be a democracy," a government team might suggest that "Education and development can only be built on the foundation of a free society." By analyzing that government point using the filter of feminism, an opposition speaker could retort with, "Unfortunately, the power dynamic drawn by Western liberalized democracies proves that they have more to gain from developing nations by continuing to coerce them into being trading partners. This is more readily established by creating the economic and political infrastructures that are congruent to their own. They act just like the cruel husband in an abusive relationship. The freedom you promise is a lie. It is an illusion to keep these nations under the thumb of Western imperialism. We demand that the developed nations leave just these poor nations alone. They are far better off without you."

There are two situations to be cautious of when using this technique. The first is getting carried away with the rhetorical criticism. Debaters can get too wrapped up in heavy analysis to the point that they lose sight of the objective. Organization should still be maintained throughout this process. The second is forgetting the links necessary between the artifact and the focal point of the debate. This is actually where synthesis comes in.

SYNTHESIS

Once an argument is broken down into several parts, it is still important to remember where all the pieces go. This is where developing a *theme*, *team line*, or team *philosophy* comes in. This is the thread that a team will use to bind all of the material together in a cohesive and encompassing fashion. This is the embodiment of external method. The way to develop and maintain a consistent line on a team will be discussed in detail in Chapter 15. It is through this integration of ideas that the most important ones are channeled together and honed into a singular concept. This is far better received by an audience than de facto forcing them to sort through the mishmash of matter scattered throughout the round.

CHAPTER 14

Internal Method

Worlds Rule 4.3.2 (a) The substantive speech of each members should include: an introduction, conclusion, and a series of arguments.

Each individual speaker has his or her own style of presentation because each has a unique personality. It should never be the goal of any teacher, coach, adjudicator, or peer to strip a debater of his or her uniqueness, but instead to help maximize his or her true potential. But there are several instances when debaters start to sound alike. They follow similar speech patterns and all seem to be oddly reading from the same script. If you try to find out where this is all rooted from, there can be no clearer culprit than having the exact same approach to internal method.

To a very large degree, it is difficult to extricate uniqueness and personal nuances when a pattern needs to be followed religiously. This pattern is a basic format that is used by every student while discovering the fundamentals of public speaking, which is to have an introduction, a body, and a conclusion. There are two areas where this becomes a problem: the inability of a speaker to break from the mold and being punished for innovation.

The mold that every beginning speaker uses is based on the same strategy employed in basic writing and composition class. It also comes from the age-old maxim, "Tell them you are going to tell them, tell them, then tell them what you told them." Like any classic story that has a "Once upon a time," then a "then they traveled far and wide," ending with "and they lived happily ever after," it is simple to follow and is easy to find all the elements involved. We know what to expect and when and where to exactly expect them. But as we grew up, it became mind-numbingly mundane to keep hearing the same set-up fairy tale after fairy tale. Wouldn't it be wonderful to hear the same fairy tales told to you by nonlinear narrative experts like Quentin Tarantino or Chuck Palahniuk?

Unfortunately, there are several traditionalists who will stand in the way of any type of innovation. They are often afraid that veering off into uncharted areas would be tantamount to abandoning the tried, true, and secure. They are both right and wrong. They are correct in assuming that traditional approaches should be measured and mastered by anyone wishing to find success in any field. But they are wrong in thinking that the basics can't be tinkered with.

Thinking that every speech is the same because each one has an introduction, a body, and a conclusion is akin to thinking that all dishes are the same because they all have ingredients. The difference among different dishes comes from the portions used, the technique employed, and the addition of spices to taste. So, sure dishes might have the same boring ingredients, but even the slightest variations can drastically change the taste and texture.

Going a bit off recipe can lead to fantastic discoveries. Just like the culinary experts on *Iron Chef* who bend the rules to bring out the unique taste they envision, if speakers are able to discover transitional techniques or learn how to master their thematic or narrative style, then it would add so much more variation and choice to their palate. But if the innovation is introduced with the wrong direction or has the wrong timing, it could be disastrous. There is a difference between bending the rules and completely breaking them.

So exactly how is this balance met? The most crucial element in learning how to improvise is first having understood the basic structure perfectly. Like any other art form, the true masters who learn how to innovate first have to study all the basics so they know when it is acceptable to go off page and know how to get back just before it goes a bit too far.

KNOWING THE LIMITS

Gauging the parameters is always the first place to start. In a classic oratorical presentation, a speech would sound something like this,

"Greetings, Ladies and Gentlemen. Today we note a problem with the status quo. We on Opening Government want to change this by adopting the following measure. My partner, the Prime Minister, introduced the measure to you and, as Deputy Prime Minister, I will further this by adding three more arguments. These are 1. This, 2. That, and 3. And the Other.

"Before we go more into depth with these arguments, allow me to provide some refutation to the points provided by the Leader of Opposition. They contend A and B. My response to A is Y. Next my response to B is Z.

"Now, let's look at the three additional arguments that I previewed more closely. 1. I am now telling you about This. 2. Now, I am telling you about That. 3. Finally, I am explaining And the Other. So, in conclusion, I am going to remind you that I proved to you that our measure should be adopted because of This, That, And the Other. Thank You."

Once again, there is nothing wrong with this structure. The parameters are quite definable. There was an obvious introduction, body, and conclusion. Here lies the problem. If you simply substitute the This, That, And the Other, A, B, Y, Z, and all the other blanks, this would be a rather dull speech. Unfortunately, after participating in a few (bad) debate rounds, you might start to think that every speech sounds like this. The good news is that this doesn't have to be the case at all. In fact, it shouldn't be.

SIGNPOSTING, TRANSITIONS, AND LINKS

Learning how to move through your speech comes from knowing how to leave enough breadcrumbs for your audience to follow. Signposting (or road mapping) is the practice of leaving marks through speech that help indicate to an audience where the speaker is in her thought process at that particular moment. The most traditional form of doing this could be found in the previous example. The use of numbers to bind the order in which the arguments are found helps the speaker maintain control and provide a constant guide to listeners. Additionally, enumerating the arguments in succession during the introduction of the speech provides the speaker with a clear-cut direction in order to make the presentation. Finally, by clearly labeling each part of the speech, the speaker is able to hold the hand of the audience and guide them through the thought process.

There is absolutely nothing wrong with signposting. In fact, this should be mandatory for all beginning debaters. But essentially relegating your speech to this format purely out of habit should never be the goal. Hearing the labels repetitively without understanding why the ideas were segregated as such does not help with the presentation. This is where transitions come in. Being able to navigate a speech by easing the audience into each new section without it being obvious or jarring is rather difficult and takes a lot of practice.

The glue that holds the whole speech together is the consistent logic that a speaker needs to thread through each point, argument, and piece of evidence. It is one thing to straight on label each of these elements, but the objective is to create a presentation that lets the elements flow naturally from one to the other. Using transitions spares the audience from listening to what could potentially be a boring, mechanical display. The barrier that should keep this in check should always be the central logic created specifically for the speech. For example, rather than saying, "There are three reasons why this measure should be moved, 1. *A*, 2. *B*, and 3. *C*," you could say, "Why exactly should this measure be moved? *A* shows us the failures of the status quo. To highlight the significant changes that will improve the situation, *B* will be explained. Finally, *C* will take us through the impacts that this will have in the whole scheme of things." It may seem much easier (and faster) to just jump into the three arguments, but transitions help the debater flesh out the ideas in a much clearer way.

If the transitions help the audience follow the speech independently, links help them connect it to the rest of the debate round. Links are necessary to establish the context from whence the speech is made vis-à-vis the other speeches in the round. These links within the speech keep the material relevant to the ongoing round and let the audience trace the steps from one thought to another. For example, if a debater made an argument that wasn't properly linked in his speech, the listener wouldn't know if it was meant to be rebuttal material (and if it was, to which argument was it responding to), positive material (that did what, exactly?), or merely part of an elaborate set-up. The structure that embraces the fully integrated use of subtle signposting, smooth transitions, and stalwart links is called **Thematic Structure**. This approach is designed as a holistic presentation that prioritizes the most important and relevant ideas in the round. It helps the debater collate similar ideas together into larger concepts. The consolidated concepts are a lot more palatable for the audience instead of expecting them to digest the smorgasbord of information being force-fed to them throughout the round. This eliminates the need for line-by-line argumentation.

The line-by-line approach was the origin for all of the tit-for–tat nonsense that dominated debating for far too long. This was the method whereby each debater created a long list of all of his or her points, and then simply enumerated them one at a time. These were rarely even clustered together and followed no particular order other than the order that they came up in the round. Then each debater would take his or her own turn by going down the list and adding his or her thoughts on each point. Matters only became worse when debaters increased their rate of speed to fit all of the ideas in as quickly as they could. This style makes sense if quantity of arguments trumps quality, which by now I hope you know is never, ever the case.

There are so many additional problems with the line-by-line technique, the first of which is an oversimplification of issues. The debaters try to tackle each point so rapidly that they inadequately develop each one and either misrepresent the ideas they are refuting and miss the point completely. As the debaters are wrapped up with trying desperately to cover every single argument, they assume that by simply mentioning jargon terms or catch phrases that they are adequately responding to points from both ends when in fact they are doing neither.

Then, since the only order followed is sequential in terms of how the points were introduced to the round, the audience is easily caught in the web of poorly connected thoughts.

On the other hand, the thematic approach allows the debater to seek the greatest common denominator between arguments and siphon the most important details imbedded within each, then funnel the processed ideas back through major themes consistent throughout the debate. This sounds a lot easier than it actually is to implement. The point here is to always go for the broader strokes, or the ideas that carry the most influence on both sides of the House. When you are prioritizing between which points to rebut from the other side, always use this maxim: Go after the point that does you the most damage. Some debaters do the opposite, opting for the arguments that are much easier to take down. This only leaves the case opposite you largely intact. If you want to take down a tree, you don't waste time going after its leaves and twigs. You must go after the roots. Yes, that is much harder to do, quite obviously. But no one ever claimed that debating was easy. This will be further evaluated in the next chapter with the discussion about creating the team line.

The border between positive material and rebuttal always seems difficult for most debaters to navigate. Even some of the most seasoned veterans and internationally renowned debaters have lost debates after making the mistake of falling too short on positive material and relying too much refutation of the opposition team. With a limited amount of time for each speech, debaters need to pick a method of prioritization that suits their style.

Worlds Rule 4.3.2(b) The substantive speech of each members should be well-timed in accordance with the time limitations and the need to prioritise and apportion time to matter.

Weaving refutation in with your case is a clever but difficult way around this. Few master this, and several have attempted to do this with uneven success. Some claim in their introduction that they will attempt to do this, and then fail to do one or the other. The only successful way of attempting this is if you have complete control of all the information brought up in the round. Then, while going through each theme in the round, evaluate each through the filter used by the side opposite, refuting their claims, then evaluating with your filter.

Meanwhile, most debaters choose to use the less-complicated approach and segregate their rebuttal material from their positive. The most popular way of accomplishing this is by presenting their introduction, then outline their case, then say, "But before I go into our case today, I am going to rebut the case of the opposition." Then, after doing this, they move on to their case and make their conclusion. As much as this seems like the formula for success, the most common problem is that debaters either get carried away with their rebuttal and fail to leave an ample amount of time for their case or, conversely, hurry through their refutation (often misrepresenting the points of the opposition) just to get to their case.

The recommended amount of time to dedicate to rebuttal is no more than two minutes during a seven-minute speech. With 30 seconds to one minute for an introduction and another 30 seconds to one minute for your conclusion, that leaves you about three to four minutes to develop your case. Throw in a couple of Points of Information and your responses to them, and you can realize just how crowded a speech can get. This is why discipline is important in taking up only the most important issues in the round. The most common error with the gravest consequence is to sacrifice your case for more rebuttal time. One way of dealing with this is using an approach developed by Canadian teams.

The *Canadian style* of refutation is when a speaker chooses to save his or her rebuttal points for the end of the speech. This permits the team to have quicker access to the positive material, leaving the rebuttal for last. This comes with a caveat. If rebuttal came first, as it typically does, then the audience still has the arguments of the opposite side fresh in their minds. With the Canadian approach, the audience's attention is now switched to your case, so rebuttal to the opposing side's case at this point might seem a bit out of place. A little reorientation by the speaker may be required.

CHAPTER 15

External Method

Australian debaters coined the terms *team line* and *team split* when referring to the process of maintaining consistency and teamwork during a debate round. In the three debaters per team, two team head to head Australian/Australasian format, there are no points of information and the speeches are six to eight minutes long. So maintaining precise structure was fundamental to success for any team. This approach translates perfectly for the Australian teams at the World Championships, where they consistently remain dominant. After observing the success derived from this style, many teams outside Oceania and Asia have tinkered with this approach and achieved similar success.

It should be noted, however, that this is not the only approach found to be permissible or, more to the point, successful. The simpler technique of building your case around a model can also be effective. It allows for more specificity and clarity in the debate. It also is far easier to defend a case the more you define the battle lines in your favor. The drawback is that you are putting all of your eggs into this basket. If you were an opening team in a round, it would be permissible for a closing team from your side to "move the debate to a deeper level and discuss the philosophical underpinnings behind the model." They could even bring in more examples that would render your case obsolete.

This is the reason why I have always recommended that teams stay away from model-driven cases. If they wish to do this, the least they could do is establish the reason why the model should be adopted. The *why* should not refer to anything accrued given a cost-benefit analysis or advantages gained from the model, etc. The *why* should be the rationale behind the agenda in the first place. Then again, if the debaters would go that far, they might as well develop a thematic structure anyway.

Worlds Rule 4.3.3 (a) The team should contain a consistent approach to the issues being debated

THE TEAM LINE

With thematic structure, the first thing that a team should develop is its team line. Understanding exactly where the point is tells the team precisely where the line in the sand should be drawn. This means that the team line/theme/philosophy should encompass all the arguments and evidence that lie squarely on that side. This helps focus on the true rationale from which all arguments will come. Something this fundamental will obviously have clearer points from which the lines for the debate should be drawn.

All four teams in a debate round should create their specific team lines. Each position would be significantly altered as the teams immediately facing against them present their own lines as well as whether they will serve to open or close their side of the house. For example, a Closing Government team would have to create a line that remained consistent with the line that the Opening Government team provided, but it also needs to address key elements that the opening team failed to present. Additionally, the Closing Government should recognize the limitations of the Opening Opposition and strategically situate itself with what it projects the Closing Opposition may do. This might sound complicated, but over time, it will become second nature.

The team line should be a rather general principle, perhaps even a statement, that directly supports or negates a first principle (depending of course on what side of the motion you find yourselves). For example, given the motion, "This House supports civilian ownership of guns," the Opening Government team in that round might say something like, "From the Government benches today, we stand behind the philosophy that the citizens of any nation should always have the right to protect themselves." The Opening Opposition might say something like, "The Opposition will stand behind the idea that the protection of a people is a responsibility that should be the sole burden of a government to bear." Closing Government may add, "Our team line from the Government today is that we should protect ourselves from the 'Nanny State'." Finally, Closing Opposition might say, "The Closing Opposition will support the philosophy that too much power to too many people is asking for too much trouble."

On their own, these are not arguments, nor do they necessarily contain the necessary elements that would help win the position on their own. They require a lot more development and direction. However, they do provide a fertile grounding from which the right ideas can grow in a specified direction. It also supports a clear distinction that would be far more recognizable and memorable to the audience and adjudicators alike.

Worlds Rule 4.3.3 (b) The team should allocate positive matter to each member where both members of the team are introducing positive matter.

THE TEAM SPLIT

With the exception of the Opposition Whip, debaters in the round must have positive material during their speeches. This means that what is brought up by the Prime Minister, Leader of Opposition, and Member of Government should not be merely parroted by their corresponding teammates. The Deputy Prime Minister and Deputy Leader of Opposition must have unique argumentation and supportive data to continue proving their side of the House.

The Government Whip has the option to provide a spilt. This remains an option since he is the final speaker from this side of the House. On one hand, it would seem that the option gives more opportunity for the Closing Government to have the "last word" as it were in the round and end its side with a bang. However, on the other hand, it opens up the possibility of the Opposition Whip providing "new refutation to the case" and tips the round in their favor. The option remains the discretion of the Closing Government team based totally on its read of the round.

No matter what the new arguments are relegated as the split are, the main point should obviously remain the same as just previously mentioned with the team line. As unique as the arguments and evidence might be for each speaker, if they are not in synch with their partner, or even worse, if they contradict their team line, it is referred to as "knifing your own partner." This is pretty disastrous in a debate and should be avoided at all costs.

On a separate but related note, as previously discussed in Chapter 5, the case should never be hung. Preparation time gives the teams the opportunity to fine-tune their cases and ensure that they are consistent and that the boundaries that they set up are not accidentally crossed, nor do they need completion from another angle before they are made independently.

A proper split demonstrates a team's ability to systematically analyze its case in a cogent and well-crafted fashion, synthesizing it through one direct and powerful philosophy that clearly distances their team from rest. It should be molded into a singular purpose, but maintain the distinctiveness and individuality of each speaker independent from the other. Much like most elements of a debate round, this is where science is overtaken by art, where experience emboldens the risk, and where practice makes perfect.

PART IV

Official Rules and Guides

World Universities Debating Championship Rules

Ray D'Cruz

PART 1—INTRODUCTION

1.1 The format of the debate

1.1.1 The debate will consist of four teams of two persons (persons will be known as "members"), a chairperson (known as the "Speaker of the House" or "Mister/Madame Speaker") and an adjudicator or panel of adjudicators.

1.1.2 Teams will consist of the following members:

1.1.3 Members will deliver substantive speeches in the following order:
   (1) Prime Minister;
   (2) Opposition Leader;
   (3) Deputy Prime Minister;
   (4) Deputy Opposition Leader;
   (5) Member for the Government;
   (6) Member for the Opposition;
   (7) Government Whip;
   (8) Opposition Whip.
       Opening Government:
       "Prime Minister" or "First Government member" and

"Deputy Prime Minister" or "Second Government member";
Opening Opposition:
"Leader of the Opposition" or "First Opposition member" and
"Deputy Leader of the Opposition" or "Second Opposition member";
Closing Government:
"Member for the Government" or "Third Government member" and
"Government Whip" or "Fourth Opposition member";
Closing Opposition:
"Member for the Opposition" or "Third Opposition member" and
"Opposition Whip" or "Fourth Opposition member".

1.1.4 Members will deliver a substantive speech of seven minutes duration and should offer points of information while members of the opposing teams are speaking.

1.2 The motion

1.2.1 The motion should be unambiguously worded.

1.2.2 The motion should reflect that the World Universities Debating Championship is an international tournament.

1.2.3 The members should debate the motion in the spirit of the motion and the tournament.

1.3 Preparation

1.3.1 The debate should commence 15 minutes after the motion is announced.

1.3.2 Teams should arrive at their debate within five minutes of the scheduled starting time for that debate.

1.3.3 Members are permitted to use printed or written material during preparation and during the debate. Printed material includes books, journals, newspapers, and other similar materials. The use of electronic equipment, with the exception of those that are exclusively dictionaries, is prohibited during preparation and in the debate.

1.4 Points of information

1.4.1 Points of Information (questions directed to the member speaking) may be asked between first-minute mark and the six-minute mark of the members' speeches (speeches are of seven minutes duration).

1.4.2 To ask a Point of Information, a member should stand, place one hand on his or her head and extend the other towards the member speaking. The member may announce that they would like to ask a "Point of Information" or use other words to this effect.

1.4.3 The member who is speaking may accept or decline to answer the Point of Information.

1.4.4 Points of Information should not exceed 15 seconds in length.

1.4.5 The member who is speaking may ask the person offering the Point of Information to sit down where the offeror has had a reasonable opportunity to be heard and understood.

1.4.6 Members should attempt to answer at least two Points of Information during their speech. Members should also offer Points of Information.

1.4.7 Points of Information should be assessed in accordance with clause 3.3.4 of these rules.

1.4.8 Points of Order and Points of Personal Privilege are not permitted.

1.5 Timing of the speeches

1.5.1 Speeches should be seven minutes in duration (this should be signaled by two strikes of the gavel). Speeches over seven minutes and 15 seconds may be penalized.

1.5.2 Points of Information may only be offered between the first minute mark and the six-minute mark of the speech (this period should be signaled by one strike of the gavel at the first minute and one strike at the sixth minute).

1.5.3 It is the duty of the Speaker of the House to time speeches.

1.5.4 In the absence of the Speaker of the House, it is the duty of the Chair of the Adjudication panel to ensure that speeches are timed.

1.6 The adjudication

1.6.1 The debate should be adjudicated by a panel of at least three adjudicators, where this is possible.

1.6.2 At the conclusion of the debate, the adjudicators should confer and rank the teams, from first placed to last placed. (see Part 5: The Adjudication)

1.6.3 There will be verbal adjudication of the debate after the first six preliminary rounds of the tournament. The verbal adjudication should be delivered in accordance with clause 5.5 of these rules.

PART 2—DEFINITIONS

2.1 The definition

2.1.1 The definition should state the issue (or issues) for debate arising out of the motion and state the meaning of any terms in the motion that require interpretation.

2.1.2 The Prime Minister should provide the definition at the beginning of his or her speech.

2.1.3 The definition must:

    (a) have a clear and logical link to the motion—this means that an average reasonable person would accept the link made by the member between the motion and the definition (where there is no such link the definition is sometimes referred to as a "squirrel");

(b) not be self-proving—a definition is self-proving when the case is that something should or should not be done and there is no reasonable rebuttal. A definition may also be self-proving when the case is that a certain state of affairs exists or does not exist and there is no reasonable rebuttal (these definitions are sometimes referred to as "truisms").

(c) not be time set—this means that the debate must take place in the present and that the definition cannot set the debate in the past or the future; and

(d) not be place set unfairly—this means that the definition cannot restrict the debate so narrowly to a particular geographical or political location that a participant of the tournament could not reasonably be expected to have knowledge of the place.

2.2 Challenging the definition

2.2.1 The Leader of the Opposition may challenge the definition if it violates clause 2.1.3 of these rules. The Leader of the Opposition should clearly state that he or she is challenging the definition.

2.2.2 The Leader of the Opposition should substitute an alternative definition after challenging the definition of the Prime Minister.

2.3 Assessing the definitional challenge

2.3.1 The adjudicator should determine the definition to be "unreasonable" where it violates clause 2.1.3 of these rules.

2.3.2 The onus to establish that the definition is unreasonable is on the members asserting that the definition is unreasonable.

2.3.3 Where the definition is unreasonable, the opposition should substitute an alternative definition that should be accepted by the adjudicator provided it is not unreasonable.

2.3.4 Where the definition of the Opening Government is unreasonable and an alternative definition is substituted by the Opening Opposition, the Closing Government may introduce matter that is inconsistent with the matter presented by the Opening Government and consistent with the definition of the Opening Opposition.

2.3.5 If the Opening Opposition has substituted a definition that is also unreasonable, the Closing Government may challenge the definition of the Opening Opposition and substitute an alternative definition.

2.3.6 If the Closing Government has substituted a definition that is also unreasonable (in addition to the unreasonable definitions of the Opening Government and Opening Opposition, the Closing Opposition may challenge the definition of the Closing Government and substitute an alternative definition.

PART 3—MATTER

3.1 The definition of matter

3.1.1 Matter is the content of the speech. It is the arguments a debater uses to further his or her case and persuade the audience.

3.1.2 Matter includes arguments and reasoning, examples, case studies, facts, and any other material that attempts to further the case.

3.1.3 Matter includes positive (or substantive) material and rebuttal (arguments specifically aimed to refute the arguments of the opposing team(s)). Matter includes Points of Information.

3.2 The elements of matter

3.2.1 Matter should be relevant, logical, and consistent.

3.2.2 Matter should be relevant. It should relate to the issues of the debate: Positive material should support the case being presented and rebuttal should refute the material being presented by the opposing team(s). The Member should appropriately prioritize and apportion time to the dynamic issues of the debate.

3.2.3 Matter should be logical. Arguments should be developed logically in order to be clear and well reasoned and therefore plausible. The conclusion of all arguments should support the member's case.

3.2.4 Matter should be consistent. Members should ensure that the matter they present is consistent within their speech, their team, and the remainder of the members on their side of the debate (subject to clauses 2.3.4, 2.3.5 or 2.3.6 of these rules).

3.2.5 All Members should present positive matter (except the final two members in the debate), and all members should present rebuttal (except the first member in the debate). The Government Whip may choose to present positive matter.

3.2.6 All members should attempt to answer at least two points of information during their own speech and offer points of information during opposing speeches.

3.3 Assessing matter

3.3.1 The matter presented should be persuasive. "The elements of matter" should assist an adjudicator to assess the persuasiveness and credibility of the matter presented.

3.3.2 Matter should be assessed from the viewpoint of the average reasonable person. Adjudicators should analyze the matter presented and assess its persuasiveness, while disregarding any specialist knowledge they may have on the issue of the debate.

3.3.3 Adjudicators should not allow bias to influence their assessment. Debaters should not be discriminated against on the basis of religion, sex, race, color, nationality, sexual preference, age, social status, or disability.

3.3.4 Points of information should be assessed according to the effect they have on the persuasiveness of the cases of both the member answering the point of information and the member offering the point of information.

PART 4—MANNER

4.1 The definition of manner

4.1.1 Manner is the presentation of the speech. It is the style and structure a member uses to further his or her case and persuade the audience.

4.1.2 Manner is comprised of many separate elements. Some, but not all, of these elements are listed below.

4.2 The elements of style

4.2.1 The elements of style include eye contact, voice modulation, hand gestures, language, the use of notes, and any other element that may affect the effectiveness of the presentation of the member.

4.2.2 Eye contact will generally assist a member to persuade an audience as it allows the member to appear more sincere.

4.2.3 Voice modulation will generally assist a member to persuade an audience as the debater may emphasize important arguments and keep the attention of the audience. This includes the pitch, tone, and volume of the member's voice and the use of pauses.

4.2.4 Hand gestures will generally assist a member to emphasize important arguments. Excessive hand movements may however be distracting and reduce the attentiveness of the audience to the arguments.

4.2.5 Language should be clear and simple. Members who use language that is too verbose or confusing may detract from the argument if they lose the attention of the audience.

4.2.6 The use of notes is permitted, but members should be careful that they do not rely on their notes too much and detract from the other elements of manner.

4.3 The elements of structure

4.3.1 The elements of structure include the structure of the speech of the member and the structure of the speech of the team.

4.3.2 The matter of the speech of each member must be structured. The member should organize his or her matter to improve the effectiveness of their presentation. The substantive speech of each members should:

    (a) include: an introduction, conclusion, and a series of arguments; and

    (b) be well-timed in accordance with the time limitations and the need to prioritize and apportion time to matter.

4.3.3 The matter of the team must be structured. The team should organize their matter to improve the effectiveness of their presentation. The team should:

(a) contain a consistent approach to the issues being debated; and

(b) allocate positive matter to each member where both members of the team are introducing positive matter

4.4 Assessing manner

4.4.1 Adjudicators should assess the elements of manner together in order to determine the overall effectiveness of the member's presentation. Adjudicators should assess whether the member's presentation is assisted or diminished by their manner.

4.4.2 Adjudicators should be aware that at a World Championship, there are many styles that are appropriate, and that they should not discriminate against a member simply because the manner would be deemed "inappropriate Parliamentary debating" in their own country.

4.4.3 Adjudicators should not allow bias to influence their assessment. Members should not be discriminated against on the basis of religion, sex, race, color, nationality, language (subject to Rule 4.2.4), sexual preference, age, social status, or disability.

PART 5—THE ADJUDICATION

5.1 The role of the adjudicator

5.1.1 The adjudicator must:

(a) Confer upon and discuss the debate with the other adjudicators;

(b) Determine the rankings of the teams;

(c) Determine the team grades;

(d) Determine the speaker marks;

(e) Provide a verbal adjudication to the members; and

(f) Complete any documentation required by the tournament.

5.1.2 The adjudication panel should attempt to agree on the adjudication of the debate. Adjudicators should therefore confer in a spirit of cooperation and mutual respect.

5.1.3 Adjudicators should acknowledge that adjudicators on a panel may form different or opposite views of the debate. Adjudicators should therefore attempt to base their conclusions on these rules in order to limit subjectivity and to provide a consistent approach to the assessment of debates.

5.2 Ranking teams

5.2.1 Teams should be ranked from first place to last place. First-placed teams should be awarded three points, second-placed teams should be awarded two points, third-placed teams should be awarded one point, and fourth-placed teams should be awarded zero points.

5.2.2 Teams may receive zero points where they fail to arrive at the debate more than five minutes after the scheduled time for debate.

5.2.3 Teams may receive zero points where the adjudicators unanimously agree that the Member has (or Members have) harassed another debater on the basis of religion, sex, race, color, nationality, sexual preference, or disability.

5.2.4 Adjudicators should confer upon team rankings. Where a unanimous decision cannot be reached after conferral, the decision of the majority will determine the rankings. Where a majority decision cannot be reached, the Chair of the panel of adjudicators will determine the rankings.

5.3 Grading and marking the teams

5.3.1 The panel of adjudicators should agree upon the grade that each team is to be awarded. Each adjudicator may then mark the teams at their discretion but within the agreed grade. Where there is a member of the panel who has dissented in the ranking of the teams, that adjudicator will not need to agree upon the team grades and may complete their score sheet at their own discretion.

5.3.2 Team grades and marks should be given the following interpretation:

Grade	Marks	Meaning
A	180-200	**Excellent to flawless.** The standard you would expect to see from a team at the Semi Final / Grand Final level of the tournament. The team has many strengths and few, if any, weaknesses.
B	160-179	**Above average to very good.** The standard you would expect to see from a team at the finals level or in contention to make to the finals. The team has clear strengths and some minor weaknesses.
C	140-159	**Average.** The team has strengths and weaknesses in roughly equal proportions.
D	120-139	**Poor to below average.** The team has clear problems and some minor strengths.
E	100-119	**Very poor.** The team has fundamental weaknesses and few, if any, strengths.

5.4 Marking the members

5.4.1 After the adjudicators have agreed upon the grade that each team is to be awarded, each adjudicator may mark the individual members at his or her discretion but must ensure that the aggregate points of the team members is within the agreed grade for that team.

5.4.2 Individual members' marks should be given the following interpretation:

Grade	Marks	Meaning
A	90-100	**Excellent to flawless.** The standard of speech you would expect to see from a speaker at the Semi Final / Grand Final level of the tournament. This speaker has many strengths and few, if any, weaknesses.
B	80-89	**Above average to very good.** The standard you would expect to see from a speaker at the finals level or in contention to make to the finals. This speaker has clear strengths and some minor weaknesses.
C	70-79	**Average.** The speaker has strengths and weaknesses and roughly equal proportions.
D	60-69	**Poor to below average.** The team has clear problems and some minor strengths.
E	50-59	**Very poor.** This speaker has fundamental weaknesses and few, if any, strengths.

5.5 Verbal adjudications

5.5.1 At the conclusion of the conferral, the adjudication panel should provide a verbal adjudication of the debate.

5.5.2 The verbal adjudication should be delivered by the Chair of the adjudication panel, or where the Chair dissents, by a member of the adjudication panel nominated by the Chair of the panel.

5.5.3 The verbal adjudication should:

5.5.4 The verbal adjudication should not exceed 10 minutes.

5.5.5 The members must not harass the adjudicators following the verbal adjudication.

5.5.6 The members may approach an adjudicator for further clarification following the verbal adjudication; these inquiries must at all times be polite and non-confrontational.

(a) identify the order in which the teams were ranked;

(b) explain the reasons for the rankings of team, ensuring that each team is referred to in this explanation; and

(c) provide constructive comments to individual members where the adjudication panel believes this is necessary.

Guide to Chairing and Adjudicating a Worlds Debate

Omar Salahuddin Abdullah, Ian Lising, Praba Ganesan and Steven Johnson

1. INTRODUCTION

This booklet is intended as a guide to assist you in performing effectively in your principal role as an adjudicator in this competition and to help you fulfill the other important responsibilities that are likely to be asked of you. These include things such as convening and chairing a debate, keeping time, conducting a post-debate adjudicators' discussion, and, finally, giving feedback and results to debaters. We understand that every experienced adjudicator will have developed an individual method for the way in which he or she runs a debate, records that debate, and gives feedback to teams and individual speakers. We are also aware that the type, quality, and duration of experience will vary considerably from one individual adjudicator to another in a tournament of this type.

2. ORAL ADJUDICATION: BACKGROUND AND OBJECTIVES

In 1998, for the first time, adjudicators were asked to give an oral adjudication, or feedback, at the conclusion of each of the first six rounds of debating (preliminaries). This feedback is designed to accomplish a number of objectives, all of these being established by Council in response to the needs of debaters as they have been expressed over the years. The first of these relates, of course, to the development of better debating. It has been a criticism of the Worlds format in the past that debaters, teams, and coaches have almost no access to the kind of constructive criticism that would allow them to hone their skills during the preliminary rounds of the competition. Moreover, teams could only guess at how well they were doing during this stage, based primarily on the kind of company in which they were debating as the early rounds progressed.

With the introduction of an oral adjudication, delivered by the Chairperson at the end of a debate, the debaters will know their finishing position (first to last) and the points (3 to 0) that they will have been awarded for that particular debate. Similarly, the adjudication will indicate how and why the adjudicators have arrived at their decision and precisely what teams and individual speakers did well and what they did not do so well (constructive criticism). The oral adjudication then provides debaters with exactly the kind of constructive criticism that they need.

The second group of objectives relates to the development and refinement of adjudication at Worlds. Oral adjudication provides an insight into the way that adjudicators observe and adjudicate debates, insight that will not only benefit debaters, but also adjudicators. The discussion leading to the decision-making stage gains a new importance as the Chair now has to advance the collective opinions of the panel in order to justify the unanimous or consensus decisions that are made when the feedback is given. This encourages all of the adjudicators on a panel to be particularly considerate and careful in the processes of observation, recording, decision making, justification, and tabulation.

3. COMPETITION ADJUDICATION

3.1 Pre-competition workshops

In every major international competition these days, all those registered as adjudicators for the duration of the competition will have to attend a seminar/workshop. It is important that you attend this seminar, even though you have a wealth of experience in Worlds adjudication. This is because the Chief Adjudicator for the competition will have certain specific things that he or she will want you to focus upon in your adjudication and, as these will differ in perspective from previous competitions that you have attended, you will need to know them, too.

Similarly, once you register as an adjudicator, you can expect to adjudicate in all of the preliminary rounds of that competition. If you are adjudicating well, and the feedback that the Chief Adjudicator's Panel is getting on your post-debate discussions is good, then you might be honored with selection to adjudicate after the break. In this light, once you register as an adjudicator, you should commit yourself to acquitting that responsibility until the Chief Adjudicator indicates that your services are no longer required. This means turning up to every briefing on time and in an appropriate physical and mental state.

3.2 Rules and regulations

As an adjudicator, you should take some to familiarize yourself with the rules of the competition. Any questions that you think you might want to ask during the seminar should be noted, no matter how silly you might think them to be. Even if you don't ask them during the seminar proper, you can always approach one of the adjudication panel immediately after the seminar is over.

3.3 Testing and accreditation

Each of these pre-competition seminars will end in an examination or test. This commonly takes the form of an adjudication of a live exhibition debate, staged there and then, or the observation and assessment of prerecorded videotape of a selected Worlds style match. At the end of the test-debate, you will be given some time to go through your notes, arrive at a decision (finishing positions) and then give your justification for this in written form. Your familiarity with Worlds Rules will also be tested. This will result in your name joining a pool of adjudicators with similar levels of skill, something that will in turn permit the Panel adjudicator in charge of the adjudicators' tab to balance the panels (members) in terms of experience and skills.

4. RUNNING THE DEBATE

4.1 Getting there

Adjudicators should get into the habit of carrying around what might be recognized as "the tools of the trade," or an adjudicator's kit, if you prefer. At the very least, this must consist of a pad of paper and a writing implement. A watch is fairly essential. You should have a digital watch if no stopwatch is available to you, just so that you can time speeches for yourself.

   You will be part of a briefing that precedes each and every round. This is your opportunity to ask the Chief Adjudicator and members of his or her panel for any further clarification of the rules, their application, and for help in solving any problems that you are having in your adjudication of your rounds. This also an opportunity to address your particular concerns to that same panel. Similarly, listen to any announcements regarding adjudication processes that are made during these briefings.

   At some time during the briefing, the match-ups will be either displayed on a screen (via OHP transparency or PowerPoint slides), or photocopies of the draw will be handed out. These lists will tell you which room you will be adjudicating in, who will be on the panel with you, and which one of you will be chairing the panel. You will also know which teams you will be adjudicating and the respective positions that they will be debating in.

The other things that you should consider, as the list of matches is revealed:

1. Whether there is a potential conflict of interests created because you have been scheduled to adjudicate your own university, or people with whom you have relationships that are likely to bias your judgment.
2. Whether you have adjudicated one or more of the teams in the forthcoming round more than twice in succession.
3. Whether there are other things that make the potential adjudication of that match difficult for you, and therefore likely to affect your adjudication of the round.
4. Raise these concerns with either the Chief Adjudicator, or one of his or her panel of deputies, as soon as you recognize them.

At the appointed time, the motion will be released to both debaters and adjudicators. You should write this down as well, checking to make sure that you have the exact wording, as it is given. Debates should commence fifteen minutes after the motion has been announced (Worlds Rulebook 3:1.3), so you should arrive at the venue of your match at least two or three minutes before that.

When the time has come for the debate to start, the Chair of the panel of adjudicators should start things off by calling teams into the room and saying something like, "I call this House to order." The Chair may then make some opening remarks.

The panel member responsible for timing speeches starts his or her watch as soon as the speaker starts speaking (not as soon as he or she stands up, clears the throat, or shuffles some papers).

4.2 Being there

From that point onwards, the debate progresses with speakers being thanked for speaking by the Chair (functioning as nominal Speaker of the House) as they conclude their speeches, and subsequent speakers being introduced by title, position or name, or combinations of these, as their turn comes to speak.

The panel member responsible for keeping time should try to give clearly audible signals (Worlds Rulebook 4:1.6). A sharp slap or knock on a flat surface (such as a table or a book-rest) with the flat of the hand will normally suffice. If a speaker begins to run overtime, it is not necessary to knock continuously, or otherwise signal that the prescribed optimum time is being exceeded. Good time management should be the responsibility of individual speakers and their teams, not the timekeeper. In this regard, it might be a good idea for the Chair of the panel to remind speakers during the opening commentary that it is acceptable for speakers to receive time signals from their teammates.

Other than these invitations, thanks, and time-signals, the adjudicators do not interfere in the debate, being involved in taking notes that detail the process and progress of the debate and observing those aspects detailed in the Worlds Rulebook 8–12: 3.1–4.4. The only time at which an interjection may become necessary from the Chair of the panel is in the event that teams or individuals are becoming unacceptably and inappropriately obtrusive during the speeches of other members. This will be times at which the members not holding the floor have begun to indulge in behavior that amounts to things like heckling, barrack-ing, and the advancement of otherwise malicious interruptions in the speech of the member holding the floor.

It should be noted that these terms are subjective and that the competition attracts many different styles of debating that are acceptable and appropriate in such a forum (Worlds Rulebook 11: 4.4.2). However, when adjudicators on a panel begin to feel that the manner of members is becoming inappropriate in such cases, then the issuance of a verbal warning to that effect, directed toward the individual, team, or bench that is behaving in such a way, allows those thus warned to amend such behavior before adjudicators begin to penalize them for the perceived breach of debating decorum. At this point, the Chair may call for "order" to be restored to the round. In this way, a clear signal is sent to those verging on the offensive and they have the option to curtail that behavior before it begins to affect their own team's manner marks.

Remember that what is, or is not, acceptable to you in this context is largely a matter of common sense, but it is better to send a clear signal to debaters in danger of overstepping these bounds before it starts affecting their marks/grades for the debate and allow them the benefit of the doubt up to that point.

If you are concerned that someone has overstepped these bounds, whether subjective or not, discuss this matter with the others on your panel at the conclusion of the debate before you reach a hard and fast conclusion.

4.3 Note-taking and making

The note-taking/making process is an important one. Not only should such notes provide you with a fairly complete description of the debate after it has been concluded, it should also present you with concrete reasons why you have reached your own particular conclusions as to how individual speakers and each of the four teams has performed. You should try to record, for example, the degree to which individuals are keeping in touch with the dynamics of the debate through things like POIs and intersections. You should also be able to indicate, within a particular speech, whether POIs have been accepted, when, what they consisted of, and how the speaker holding the floor at the time responded to them.

You should also be able to track the logic and flow of an argument or idea through your own notation and determine whether statements have been left largely unsupported (asserted) (Worlds Rulebook 8: 3.3), whether speeches have a reasonable balance and are consistent (Worlds Rulebook 8: 3.3.3–3.3.4), and whether speakers have misrepresented things said earlier in the debate, among other things.

An individual adjudicator's approach to note taking is likely to be markedly different from person to person. The main thing is that you develop a means of accurately charting what has happened in the debate.

4.4 The observation process

The observation process is also important. You should be watching how readily a speaker's manner develops a rapport with the audience (if any, or your panel, if not), how she or he stands, gesticulates, and is expressive during the delivery of his or her speech. Similarly, you should watch for things such as how members not holding the floor continue to communicate with each other during the course of the debate and maintain contact with it through the POI and more general interaction (appropriate reactions to statements being made, laughter, etc.).

4.5 Conclusion of the round

When the last speaker has concluded his or her remarks and retaken his or her seat, it is customary for the Speaker, or Chair of Adjudicators (in the event that he/she is taking the role of the Speaker of the House), to give the debaters "permission to cross the house." This is so that teams can shake hands and congratulate each other on a successful debate.

It is pertinent at this point to tell members that they can withdraw while a decision is made by adjudicators, in which case they must all withdraw until asked to return to the room.

5. THE DECISION-MAKING PROCESS

5.1 The integrity of opinions, decisions, and processes

Either way, the discussion that is then held between adjudication panel members is confidential, and its course and specifics should not be made known to individual debaters. This confidentiality is essential if adjudicators are to maintain a degree of professionalism, and neither to undermine, nor be undermined by, their fellow adjudicators.

Consensus decisions are exactly that. Different adjudicators see debates in different ways. That's exactly why we have panels of adjudicators. However, we should avoid making individual perceptions about a particular debate, or a particular adjudicator, common knowledge. This in no way restricts the kind of advice that you may be asked for by a particular speaker or team; it merely asks of you that you are considerate of your colleagues in advancing your own comments and suggestions.

5.2 Arriving at a decision

At the end of the debate, your panel begins the process of discussion and decision making. While the following is not presented as either a schedule or a checklist for this process, it is clear that these major components will each have to feature somewhere in the process of your deliberations.

5.3 Time to reflect

The first thing that should happen, after the debaters, audience, and television crew (it happens!) have left the room, is that the panelists should take a few minutes to review their notes before any form of discussion begins. During this "quiet time" individual panelists should highlight items, arguments, comments, and so on, that they consider being critical in terms of the debate, its outcomes and their respective decisions.

1. Don't let any of your preconceptions or individual knowledge on the motion affect the outcome of the round. It is absolutely unacceptable for a judge to say, "If I were in the round, this is what I would have said. And since they failed to bring that up, they should be penalized for it." Your decision should not be based on what wasn't or what should have been what said, but ONLY on what was said by the debaters during the round.
2. Don't let any of your preconceptions about the degree of difficulty imposed by the wording of the motion on teams (on either side) create notions of sympathy that then bias your grading in their favor (or against them).
3. Do consider each team (and speaker) as having a specific range of roles that he or she must fulfill in the debate. Teams and speakers have responsibilities and roles that are often markedly different, but nonetheless vital, to the successful progress of a debate.
4. Don't lose sight of the balance in an individual speech. There should be a natural and appropriate portion of time devoted to definitions, rebuttal arguments, the development of arguments in support of a case, summaries, and responses to questions and challenges. A speaker who spends six minutes haranguing the opposition and only starts on his or her portion of the split as the second single knock of the gavel sounds is not delivering a very balanced speech! Keep an eye on the watch as speakers move through transitions from one phase of a speech to another. Not all speakers will "signpost" these transitions, but you must endeavor to recognize them anyway.
5. Do continually test arguments for their logical development, relevance to the case being presented (or argued against), and the validity of any support (examples, models, statistics, etc.) that is delivered in respect of these arguments.
6. Don't ignore cries of misrepresentation, squirreling, self-serving definitions, slides, and so on. Check these claims against your notes before you judge them to have been validly or invalidly made.

7. Do enjoy the debate, but don't communicate anything specific to the debaters as you observe it and take notes. This is sometimes as innocent as an inadvertent nod of the head at the moment that a speaker advances the weakest argument in the history of parliamentary debating, but the apparently duplicitous nod suddenly makes it appear to be potentially the best one, and suddenly the whole complexion of the debate changes. The key here is to be sufficiently conscious of your own body language and reactions to keep them consistent with the kind of normal reaction that a speaker is trying to evoke (laughter, seriousness, etc.).

8. Don't get too caught up with technicalities, minor infringements of the rules as you interpret them, or pet likes and dislikes. You should be viewing the debate from the macro-level as much as from the level of its sophistication, its intricacies, and technical complexity. An adjudicator who penalizes a speaker for "... gesticulating with his left hand too much," or wearing a blouse that clashes with her handbag is definitely missing the point somewhere.

5.4 Panel decisions

1. Panel decisions are final.
2. Panels have to place the four teams in the debate round, as first, second, third, and fourth. First-ranked team has won the round, and the fourth-ranked team has finished last in the debate round.
3. No two teams can be placed in the same rank.
4. The total team scores must reflect the rankings of the team, and no two teams should have the same total team scores.
5. A consensus decision is when all members of the panel agree on the rank of a team.
   o A complete consensus decision is when every single team rank has been decided through a series of consensus decisions among the panel members. The panel therefore had complete unanimity over all the team ranking decisions.
6. A majority decision is when a majority of the panel members agree on the rank of a team.
   o A complete majority decision is when every single team rank has been decided only by majority decisions.
7. A partial consensus–majority decision is when the panel is in consensus over some rank/s and made majority decisions over the other rank/s.
8. There can be either a complete consensus decision, a complete majority decision, or a partial consensus–majority decision.
9. A panel should discuss all pertinent issues of the debate adequately and deal with all concerns of panel members.

10. Chairs have the discretion to end discussions on particular issues or on the whole debate, if they find the discussion to cease being constructive or not progress.

5.5 Panel members

1. Members should contribute constructively, and the chair of the panel is obliged to promote fair exchange of ideas on the debate among panel members.
2. Panel members should provide their brief read of the debate, focusing on their main concerns and observations before the panel tries to reach a decision.
3. Panels are encouraged to arrive at a consensus; however, the final decision to cast a vote is the privy of individual panel members. Panel members should vote according to their conscience, and not according to expediency.
4. A panel member can shift positions on an issue or the whole debate during/after the discussion process, because the discussion has convinced him or her it is appropriate to shift position. Panel members are warned not to shift positions purely because of the experience, reputation, and intimidation of any panel members or panel chair.

5.6 Chair of panel

1. Assumes the role of facilitator, mediator, and leader of panel.
2. Has NOT failed to fulfill his or her role if there is no complete consensus decision or if he or she finds him- or herself in the minority of a majority decision.
3. Should encourage panel members to offer their opinions or observations of the debate.
4. Has to respect the views of all members of the panel.
5. Should organize the thread of discussion in order to cover all concerns of panel members as much as possible.
6. Use discretion when ending a discussion on a particular issue or the debate as a whole, and resort to a vote.

5.7 Agreeing on grades for speakers and teams

Panelists should then move on to confer on grades for teams and speakers. You should reach agreement on these things if you can, because it makes the work of the tabulation crew that much less complicated, and they can look forward to living longer and more productive lives. While the rules allow for a degree of flexibility within the grade bandwidths that you have already decided upon, you've managed to achieve consensus thus far, so why not push your luck a little further!

One way to approach this is to try and agree on the standard of the debate as a whole. As the power-matching software starts to spread things out nice and evenly after about round three, you should find this progressively easier to do as the competition goes on, because there should be an increasing level of similarity in the strengths and skills of teams debating in each match. Remember that you still have a little flexibility within a particular grade (or band) in terms of the marks that can be awarded to an individual speaker, so you can still use this range to reflect your own opinions. However, remember also that the marks of the two speakers, when added together, must still equate with the overall grade that has been agree for the team.

5.8 Filling in adjudication sheets

At this point, the panelists can begin to fill in their adjudication sheets, with perhaps one last communal check through what has been agreed and what the final decision is, just to make absolutely sure. It may also be a good idea at this stage for the Chair to ask for any points that the panelists would like incorporated into the oral adjudication of the debate.

1. Decide on finishing positions.
2. Fill in the Speed Ballot form [Chair].
3. Check that the Speed Ballot has been filled in correctly [Panelists].
4. Summon a "runner."
5. Send the Speed Ballot off to the Tab Room.
6. Decide team grades.
7. Contribute and summarize points to be included in the feedback.
8. Call teams back into the room.
9. Commence the oral adjudication.
10. Fill in the adjudication sheets, completing all mark and grade boxes and appending comments where relevant or required.
11. Give all the completed forms to a runner before you leave the room, floor or area.
12. Once members have settled again, the Chair will then begin the oral adjudication

6. EVALUATING COMPETING LINES OF ARGUMENT

While the broad categories of "matter" and "manner" serve as touchstones for evaluation, they focus mainly on assessing the qualities of an individual's performance in the round. Manner is concerned with the style and structure of a speaker's presentation—delivery, organization, and language use—while matter is concerned with the content and analysis of an individual's presentation—that a speaker's arguments are relevant, logical, and consistent with his or her team's or side's positions.

While useful, these categories do not provide the adjudicator guidance on how to weigh competing lines of argument. Although the adjudication of a Worlds round does not require that the adjudicators declare a winning "side" in the debate, the debaters involved will almost unfailingly be concerned with whether the Government or Opposition prevailed on the question. Moreover, successful adjudication of a round in the Worlds style—that is, the ranking of teams from best to worst—must be concerned with the comparison of each team's positions relative to the other teams' positions.

Adjudicators, both when adjudicating the debate and when articulating the panel's decision to the debaters in the oral adjudication, should pay particular attention to three elements of the argument: the issue over which the debate is contested; the standard by which the arguments on either side of the issue may be assessed; and the appraisal of each team's arguments relative to that standard.

6.1 Identifying the issue

All debates may be characterized as a clash of arguments over an issue—some statement that serves as the ideological dividing line between Government and Opposition argumentative ground. Identifying the issue in a debate is the first step toward successfully adjudicating the competing arguments in the round.

Ideally, the issue is made clear early in the debate, either by the motion or by the Government. The majority of Worlds-style debates will have as their central issue the motion as announced. This is particularly true when the motion is exceptionally clear: "This House believes that making Yassar Arafat a partner in peace was a mistake" or "This House would make company directors criminally liable for the wrongs of their companies" are examples of motions that define clear ground for the Government and Opposition and, therefore, serve as the primary issue in the debate.

Other motions are less useful as issue statements. Motions that allow the Government room to interpret the topic and define the focus of the debate are less likely to function as issue statements. A motion such as "This House believes that religious leaders should listen to public opinion" may be supported by a general case in which a Government offers arguments that clergy should be responsive to their followers, or it may motivate a Government to run a specific case that is derived from the motion. When presented with the motion above, for example, the Government could choose to run a case that argues the Catholic church should be more proactive in acknowledging and addressing issues of sexual abuse of minors by Catholic priests. When the Government chooses to define a case that is more specific than the motion offered, the central issue in the round typically is the thesis of the case offered by the Government, not the motion itself.

While the issue statement will usually be explicit in the round, there will be cases in which neither side makes apparent the central issue in the round. In this case, the adjudicator must articulate an issue as a starting point for his or her adjudication. When doing so, an adjudicator should phrase an issue statement that is clear and balanced. To be clear, an issue statement should define ground for both the Government and Opposition team in a way that makes obvious their responsibilities. A balanced issue statement will avoid expressing the controversy in a way that might be weighted toward one side or the other.

6.2 Determining the appropriate standard for evaluation

In all decisions, the adjudicator will utilize some criterion or criteria to make his or her assessment of the arguments advanced by the debaters. For example, when adjudicating a debate on the motion "This House believes the International Monetary Fund has done more to harm than help the global condition," an adjudicator must be able to determine how to evaluate relatively the instances of the IMF "harming" and "helping" the global condition as argued by the debaters. Should impact to local economies be prioritized over facilitating the transition to a global economy? Should concern for effects on the environment and workers' rights be subjugated to the long-term benefits of capitalism? How should the deterioration of state sovereignty be weighed against the benefits of global trading opportunities?

The issue statement for the debate will usually contain some term or phrase that will serve as the standard for evaluating the competing arguments of each side. This term or phrase typically expresses some evaluation of the subject under consideration. Consider the previously mentioned motion: "This House believes that making Yassar Arafat a partner in peace was a mistake." In this example, the term that proposes an evaluation of Arafat's performance is "mistake." In other words, to evaluate the competing arguments in the round, the adjudicator will employ as his or her standard whether the examples of Arafat's performance offered by each side constitute a "mistake." For this term to function as a standard, the adjudicator must know what constitutes a "mistake." For the IMF motion, the adjudicator must understand what is meant by "the global condition" before he or she may determine which side has best substantiated the impact of the IMF on the global condition. Thus, the nature and definition of the "global condition" becomes the standard for evaluating the competing arguments.

In an ideal situation, the debaters would make clear the standard to be used to weigh competing arguments in the round. The definition of the pertinent term or phrase would be made clear by the Government side and their all arguments would be made relevant to that definition. Similarly, the Opposition would recognize the Government's definition and orient its arguments toward that standard as well. For example, if "mistake" in the Arafat motion was defined as "anything that has served to impede the progress toward peace," both the Government and Opposition would align their arguments for Arafat's influence with an eye toward proving that his presence has affected—either positively or negatively—the progress toward peace.

More typically, however, both sides in a round will have competing standards for evaluating their arguments. With the IMF motion, the Government may defend the escalating Gross Domestic Product of IMF beneficiaries while the Opposition may argue that the austerity measures imposed by the IMF cause significant damage to social programs. Without a clear standard advanced by either side, the adjudicator is left to decide how to evaluate these competing positions. In cases where the respective sides in the debate have failed to "agree" on a particular standard, the adjudicator must determine the standard for evaluating the competing arguments.

When determining a standard, the adjudicator should acknowledge the Government's responsibility to define the terms of the motion. Assuming that the Government has defined the terms, particularly the term or phrase that will serve as the standard for the competing arguments, some presumption should be given their definition regardless of whether the Opposition chooses to orient its arguments toward that standard. The criteria of clarity and balance applied to the issue statement are also relevant to the definitions offered by the Government: Any definition of a standard should increase the clarity of the debate and should not exclude the potential for Opposition argument.

Frequently, however, the Government will fail to define the pertinent term or phrase and the adjudicator will be required to extract a standard for evaluation from the arguments made by both sides in the debate. In the IMF example, the arguments that a beneficiary country's GDP has improved following IMF intervention and that austerity measures have had a detrimental impact on the social welfare of a country may both be true. The adjudicator must then decide how to compare the competing arguments. Ideally, the debaters will give cues on how to do so in their own argumentation. In this instance, the arguments relevant in the round are focused on the effect of IMF involvement on the beneficiary country. While this may not evaluate the consequences of IMF actions on "the global condition" as most would understand the "global condition" (i.e., as more broad reaching than the effect of the IMF on a single country) it is what the debaters have opted to focus on. To penalize either side for failing to make the arguments the adjudicator believes would be most appropriate is not sound adjudication.

In such a case, directed by the arguments the debaters have made, the adjudicator may extract a standard of "impact to the beneficiary country." He or she would then evaluate competing arguments about the benefits or harms of IMF involvement from the perspective of how those outcomes may affect a beneficiary country.

6.3 Appraising the arguments

Once a standard has been determined, the adjudicator must compare the arguments made in the round to that standard. At this point, the adjudicator should appraise each argument for its relevance to the standard. That relevance may be measured in two ways.

Initially, relevance may be measured from a quantitative perspective. The adjudicator may appraise a side's arguments for the impact the totality of those arguments has on the standard. More positions relevant to the standard, using a strict quantitative perspective, mean that a particular side should prevailed. If the Government offers five examples of how Arafat's presence has diminished the prospects for peace to the Opposition's two examples of how Arafat has improved the prospects for peace, the Government would likely prevail. This perspective, however, has limited utility on its own.

Arguments must also be appraised from a qualitative perspective in which the adjudicator assesses the significance of each argument's impact to the standard. Some examples or arguments will be more relevant the standard than others. Building off the previous example, the adjudicator may believe that the two arguments offered by the Opposition are more relevant to the standard—perhaps those two examples of how Arafat benefited the peace process were very detailed and specific whereas the Government's five examples of Arafat's detractions from the peace process were vague and ill developed. In this case, the Opposition would likely prevail.

Thus, a Worlds round might have a team present seven arguments, but have the opposing team address all of them sufficiently with just one. The most important point here is that the adjudicator account for each major line of argument advanced by the Government and Opposition and assess the merit of each of those arguments relative to the standard.

6.4 Conclusion

This approach to adjudication of the round is most useful for clearly articulating a basis for decision in a verbal adjudication. Verbal adjudications may be structured around these three concepts quite simply.

The Chair of a panel may open an oral adjudication by identifying the issue that divided the Government and Opposition ground in the debate; this may be as simple as saying "The central issue in the round was whether involving Arafat in the peace process was a mistake." From there, the Chair would articulate the panel's consensus as to the standard employed for evaluating the competing lines of argument: "The Panel understood that whether Arafat's involvement would be considered a mistake depended upon whether he had contributed to or detracted from the peace process." Finally, the Chair would sort through the major lines of argument advanced by each side to offer an appraisal of those each of those arguments relative to this standard.

An oral adjudication structured around these concepts will provide the debaters with the certainty that each of their respective arguments was weighed in the adjudicators' consideration. That certainty will, in turn, demonstrate that the adjudicators were discharging their duties responsibly.

7. THE ORAL ADJUDICATION

As with things like note taking, individual adjudicators will each have his or her own way of giving an oral adjudication.

7.1 Announcing positions

There is a division of opinion over whether it is best to announce results first and then give the feedback, or whether to give the feedback first and then announce the result. Our advice would be to adopt the former method, because it is questionable how much benefit teams and speakers can get if they are anxiously waiting for the result and you are, unconsciously perhaps, trying to give nothing away.

7.2 Opening remarks

You may like to preface your remarks with a few comments on the quality and standard of the debate (coming from your discussions on an overall debate grade?). You may also indicate whether there was a unanimous agreement, or whether the panel encountered some resolvable disagreements in the course of its discussion (thereby indicating that the match might well have been very close in some respects).

7.3 The Framework and content of your feedback

As with the set-up for a debater's speech, an adjudicator's feedback should have matter and manner. You should also structure your own intended feedback. Give the finishing order, from team placing first in the debate (and therefore winning it) to that placing last.

7.4 The overview

Then, proceed with the overview of the debate that your panel has assembled during your discussions, but keep it brief. Focus on the definition, the parameters and demands that this set up, the cases and major arguments that followed this, the challenges that these represented, and the way that these challenges were met. You should be able to trace the major issue(s) or themes that ran through the debate through this overview, as well as focusing on the ways in which various teams dealt with these.

7.5 Relative merits of teams, roles, cases, argumentation, etc.

It would then be a good idea to explain exactly why the debate has been awarded to a particular team and consider the positions of the other teams relative to this. The reasons why teams have finished in the particular order that you have determined should then follow, with the relevant explanations offered as you go. You should conclude this phase by summarizing what you have said, but by means of reference to the key arguments and issues that you outlined in your opening commentary. Comments about eye contact, off-key humming, and torn jeans are probably not appropriate at this point.

7.6 Concluding

Your adjudication feedback might then move toward a conclusion with any specific comments on the roles, performance, and style of individual speakers being offered. However, this should only be necessary in the event that an individual's speech has affected the debate, or a team's role, in a particularly critical way. Please try to keep your remarks in these cases constructively critical, perhaps softening what might be construed as negative criticism by picking out some positive aspects as well and mentioning them.

8. CONCLUSION

The main thing is that you enjoy the experience of adjudicating at Worlds and profit from this in the context of your own development as an adjudicator and perhaps even as a debater. It comes down to one thing: common sense. If you continually apply that particular quality to the process of running, observing, discussing, and assessing the debates that you will see, it will not only be you that gains. The debaters, the organizers, and the competition that is Worlds Universities Debating will profit too.

THE ADJUDICATION CHECKLIST

1. The phases of a debate adjudication: Observing the debate (which includes chairing and time-keeping if necessary), discussion of the debate (a session led by the chair of the panel), and giving the oral adjudication (announce decision, provide reasons for decision, and offer advice to debaters). The final phase is excluded for the final three preliminary rounds and the final series.
2. Observing the debate
   o Chairing the debate also includes the responsibility of keeping order in the debate, inviting speakers to speak, and cautioning against inappropriate behavior when warranted.
3. Discussing the debate
   o Matter and Manner contribution of each team should be discussed (along with Points of Information, as in the quality of the questions and the responses to them, which contain both manner and matter elements).

- o All members of the panel are obliged to provide their read of the debate and listen to the various views of the other members of the panel.
- o Chairs of panel should drive the discussion and attempt to move it forward. Use their discretion to end dead discussions and allow all panel members equal access to the discussion.

4. Oral Adjudication
   - o Presented by the chair of the panel, or a member of the majority, if the chair is dissenting.
   - o Announce the rankings before explaining the verdict (encouraged), if not the explanation would ambiguous and not constructive.
   - o Explain to the debaters, why the panel/majority decided the team ranking in that order, so debaters can understand how the adjudicators distinguished the teams in terms of contribution and delivery.
   - o Provide constructive advice (drawn collectively from the panel) for the debaters.

Guide to Bidding, Planning, and Running a *World Universities Debating Championship*

Ian T. Lising

I.   **SHOULD WE BID TO HOST WORLDS?**

Deciding to host a World Universities Debating Championships (WUDC or Worlds) is (to put it mildly) a life-altering event. The inaugural Championship was hosted by the Glasgow University Union in January 1981 with 50 teams from eight nations competing. Since then it has dramatically expanded to an event that hosts over 350 teams from 150 universities of 40 nations. Worlds has been patronized and supported by several world leaders and sponsored by several transnational corporations.

That does sound a bit daunting. Perhaps this is the time where most people feel intimidated and think to themselves, "You must absolutely mad to take on something like that." Although that may be partially true, this guide is meant to dispel the myths, spark ideas, and provide general direction to those who are willing to take on the task of hosting Worlds.

Before we get into any of that, the first question that comes to mind usually is:

1.   What do we get from hosting Worlds?

Hosting Worlds is neither something you decide to do on a whim nor a responsibility you take on if you lose a bet. You will undoubtedly risk several sleepless months, fractured relationships, and other personal losses. But in the end, it could lead to tremendous international recognition and an opportunity for your debating organization, university, community, nation, and region to experience Worlds firsthand in one glorious week.

a. International recognition

No, not for you (although that does come for some from time to time), but international recognition will be earned for your debating organization, university, and nation. Offhand, this might sound shallow to some. But its impact is far deeper than they would first think.

Much like the universities they represent, debating organizations are only as successful as their reputation permits them to be. It is a sad notion, but unfortunately true. No matter what successes you enjoy over a debating career, short of winning Worlds, people tend to forget. Each year, only two universities' names go down on the permanent history of the Championship, the winner and the host. Trust me, hosting is the more realistic venture of the two.

b. Immediate Worlds exposure

If you have participated at Worlds, you often feel the need to share the experience with others as soon as you return home. My family knew that I would fly to some exotic locale around Boxing Day and miss the holidays every year, but that was the extent of their Worlds experience. The same is true unfortunately for everybody else in your region, country, university, and even debating organization. Each year, I take my students to Worlds, and those new to the experience always say the same thing, "I had no idea it would be like this." No matter how many debates you participate in, there is nothing quite like Worlds.

This is where hosting changes everything. When we hosted Worlds at Ateneo de Manila in 1999, there were high school students who worked as volunteers, sat in audiences, and even joined some events during the week. Several of them went on to have their own fantastic debating careers. National media helped us reach a much larger audience and the impact of that is immeasurable. Debating culture in the Philippines became something tangible.

After hosting Worlds, the Ateneo Debate Society was able to built on that success and take it much further. The same could be said of Stellenbosch 1997, Nanyang 2004, etc. The general interest in debating can be more easily piqued if the venue is somewhere closer to home. Sharing Worlds with the upcoming generation of your debating organization would be the best way to ensure its future.

2. What is our timetable for the bid?

The first thing you must do is to determine what type of experience your organization has in running a major international intervarsity debating tournament. Have you hosted a local, national, or even regional IV? It would be wise to start here first. Build your way up the ladder until you are able to get some experience with smaller-scaled events.

You must also take into consideration that your organization must have dedicated members who have been to a few international intervarsity tournaments and who will be at your institution for a few years to come. This may be the more difficult task given that the soonest that the Worlds you'd run would be two and a half years from the time that you first decided to do it. So if you have a crop of committed second-years/sophomores/undeclared-majors-who-will-undoubtedly-overstay, then you are in business.

a. Getting university support

Convincing your college/university/institution to host this prestigious event might sound academic, but don't fool yourself. If the administration is not unquestionably supportive and enthusiastic about the bid (i.e., if they use language like, "Well, that sounds nice," or "What's Worlds?") then you might reconsider.

Without the total support, your work will be that much more difficult. Some institutions have even gone to the extreme of charging their very own organizing committee for the use of their classrooms during the tournament. Set up meetings with your institutional president as well as the deans, chancellors, department chairs, and faculty. The more people you have behind you, the better. Make sure that you fully communicate the gravity of the event and how it will infinitely benefit the institution.

b. Getting community/corporate support

If you were extremely lucky, you would be attending a university that will fully fund your Worlds and all of its needs. Now, wake up, because that is never going to happen. The university may take lead sponsorship (if you have some luck), but most institutions will just say that they "support" the idea and leave it at that. This means that you must find other financial measures for the bid. If your university has a lot of donor support, then you could persuade your administration to help set up a meeting. This will ensure compatibility with your sponsor and the institution. There have been several tournaments where this was not the case and it led to, well, complications.

Make sure that if you are lucky to land a business that is willing to go in as the title sponsor that your contracts are in order. It would be smarter to have them fix their pledge expressed in stable currencies. After our bid in January 1997, we suffered under the strain of the Asian-currency crisis and the worth of our committed budget was halved. Be very careful with all of your contracts.

Title sponsors may also enforce exclusivity clauses that will invariably hamper your ability to find other sponsors. In other words, if you find a willing giant, make sure it commits an ample amount worthy of its reputation and your need.

c. Getting materials prepared

The initial bid document has come in several forms, ranging from flashy, colorful ones that are professionally printed on glossy brochures worthy of being framed, or simple black-and-white text forms with no photographs, and everything else in between. How much money you decide to spend on the document that will be scrutinized by the members of the World Debating Council is really up to you. I must be honest, though. Take time to ensure that every detail on the copies you hand out is completely accurate. Do not make promises that you cannot keep. Be realistic with what you are offering.

The bid document must include a short history about your institution and debating organization. You may include a short national bit if you wish. It should include support letters from the institution and, if you have them, letters of support from your sponsors. You should include the events that you are planning as well as your proposed logistical schematic. This means that you would have to estimate how much Worlds would cost and how you plan to cover it.

You must have projected registration fee as well as probable residence facilities. If you are fortunate to have suitable on-campus accommodations that will be vacant for the duration of the event, then plan on using them. Melbourne 1994, Stellenbosch 1997, and Sydney 2000 all had fantastic on-campus facilities that worked wonderfully. Of course, they had to carefully plan and execute information desks, food distribution, medical needs, communication, amenities, etc.

If you don't have on-campus vacancy for the duration of Worlds, find out if you have a major hotel (or two nearby ones) and determine what the maximum capacity would be. At the institution, find the area that you plan to use as your briefing room and estimate its full capacity. These will help you determine what your maximum team capacity will be. Always remember to cap the number of teams per institution before you turn away entire institutions. Worlds is about inclusion. But remember, shooting for "the Biggest Worlds ever" will NEVER make it the "BEST Worlds ever."

Estimate the expected travel time from the hotel, event locations, and the campus as well as the means (i.e., buses/walking). Toronto 2002 issued the tournament ID cards that doubled as free passes on its public transportation system for the whole week. You may not be able to pull off something magical like that, but the foresight and little touches like that will make the difference between a decent Worlds and a legendary one.

3. Who do we need to be on our Bid Team?

Typically, the same people who are intending to do the heavy lifting for Worlds would be the exact same ones making all of the promises at Council. The bid presenter should be the intended Convenor for the tournament. Some bid presentations in the past have been made by the Chief Adjudicator (CA). This would be fine if the proposed CA is directly connected to the bidding institution and will be with the hosts for entire duration. Council members usually get nervous about placing their vote with a personality who changes with each segment of the bid process. Consistency is the key for building trust with the council members. So the bottom line is, the bid presenter must be articulate, trustworthy, have a significant role with the organizing committee, and be present at every stage of the bid process and throughout the running of the event.

a. The Convenor/Championship Director

Often mistaken for the most obsessive and control freakish of the lot, the Convenor or Championship/Tournament Director will primarily be the face of Worlds. As daunting as this position may seem, some Worlds have segregated the role into two or even three positions. But the function is to be the focal person to manage and direct Worlds at every stage. It is ideal that the proposed convenor has been to more than one Worlds before the bid process begins. There have been a couple of instances where a Worlds rookie stood before council as the proposed Convenor and those Worlds turned out fine. But the more experience that the Convenor has with what Worlds is supposed to be like, the better. The Convenor should have an outgoing spirit and know how to manage and trust his or her team.

b. The Chief Adjudicator

The proposed Chief Adjudicator should have adjudicated in at least one Worlds before joining the bid process. It would be a good idea to have a CA who is very familiar with the organizing committee. But there have been a few occasions when the CA was not student/faculty/alumnus of the proposed host school. In fact, there has been at least one Worlds where the CA was from a different country altogether. It is crucial to have a CA who is exceptionally respected as an adjudicator in at least his or her country and region. However impossible at certain circumstances, it would be highly advisable to have a CA who is widely known and greatly respected throughout the Worlds circuit.

c. Worlds Delegates

It is also very critical that a strong buzz is created during the tournament even before the bid presentation takes place. This means that all of the debaters and adjudicators from the proposed host should act as ambassadors of the bid committee at all times. It would be equally helpful to get the support of all the national and regional delegates present. Often, the proposed host delegates would wear t-shirts, jumpers, jerseys, or any other paraphernalia bearing their Worlds teams during the tournament and as they stand in for support at the bid presentation. The delegates should be briefed about the basic information and be ready to answer questions informally as they are most certain to come.

4.   How does the Bid Process work?

The formal process of announcing the bid goes through the World Council Chair. You should contact the Chair two months before Worlds at the very latest. Technically, you could just show up at the pre-council meeting on the 27th and announce your intentions then, but that would not be such a great idea. Potential bid competitors creating their buzz months ahead of you would put you at a huge disadvantage coming in. Additionally, a seemingly last minute presentation doesn't give the appearance of a serious bid. The Chair will formally announce your bid when he or she posts the agenda for the upcoming World Council Meeting. This is usually done online through the various debating list serves.

If you wish to generate your own fanfare prior to the announcement, it will help you gauge what reactions you might have (especially from your region). This inevitably helps you determine if you will have the support of everyone you need it from. It has also become rather in vogue to create a website for the bid. It is recommended to find formal online addresses. A Facebook or Myspace page will not reflect the seriousness of your endeavor. Usually, a space provided by your institution website demonstrates the support that you are receiving from them. The site will become indispensable if you win the bid.

At Worlds, bidders are allowed to hand out all of the paraphernalia that they wish to Council members at the pre-council meeting typically held on the afternoon of the 27th of December. They are not allowed to make announcements nor are they allowed to field questions at the meeting, but they are welcomed to sit in during the proceedings. At the conclusion of the pre-council meeting, bidders are allowed to introduce themselves informally to the council delegates and field questions as they wish. The formal bid presentation is reserved for the main Council meeting on the 1st of January.

a.   Knowing your competition

It is but natural to feel competitive with any other university that wishes to bid at the same year that you have been long preparing for. But you must resist the urge to engage in silly confrontational tactics as you try desperately to undermine the competition. Typically, this usually backfires. Knowing what your competitor is offering and making sure that you cover your own bases is far more effective and constructive in the long run.

b.   Do we really need our DCAs now?

No. It may be true that all bidders should always have their ducks in a row, but naming the Deputy Chief Adjudicators at the initial bidding stage is not one of the steps that I would recommend. Yes, it is critical to have all the proposed DCAs there for the bid confirmation a year later, but this early in on the process, it is unlikely that you will find Worlds personalities who could positively guarantee that they will be available two years later. To illustrate the point, during the

Ateneo de Manila 1999 initial bid presentation at the Council meeting in Stellenbosch 1997, I was announced as the proposed Chief Adjudicator. A year later, circumstances required me to shift roles to Championship Director. Things happen, situations change, and DCAs will almost certainly not have the ability to secure a full commitment that far in advance.

c.   Pre-Council materials

Most bidders will hand out the official bid document at the pre-council meeting. This must include all the plans and letters of commitment that you received at this point. Letters of support from your university and sponsors will give council members a sense of how serious you are about the prospects of hosting Worlds and that your institution and community are willing to share the responsibility. Commitment letters from hotels may be a little more difficult to obtain at this point, but the logistical blueprints for the entire event should be included. Be certain that you will not make promises that you can't keep. The purpose of handing out materials at the pre-council meeting is to give the council delegates an opportunity over the next few days to consult with their contingents and fellow nationals with all the information available. Once again, no formal statements or announcements should be made at this time. The handouts should just be simply distributed. They are welcomed to hand out other paraphernalia if they wish, but most save it for the main council meeting.

d.   New Year's day

One of the toughest things to do is to spend your New Year's day sitting through the quagmire that is the World Debate Council. While the rest of Worlds enjoys the free day touring the city, nursing their hangovers, and catching up with the week's lost sleep, council members will find themselves stuck in a conference room for about 12 glorious hours. The bid presentations are usually held during the first part of the council meeting after the final report from the preceding Worlds, the initial report of the current Worlds, and the confirmation report of the next year's host. This is a good opportunity for the bidders to observe the process that every Worlds host goes through. Then, there is usually a coin-toss or other simple mechanism to determine bid presentation order. After each presentation, a question and answer period is allotted. Finally, voting takes place and the winning bid is announced.

II.   GREAT, WE WON THE BID! NOW WHAT DO WE DO?

Congratulations. Here's where the fun begins. After all of the necessary announcements and celebration, work starts in earnest. Some winning bids think that the bulk of the work happens a few days before the Mid-Year Report is due in July, but the truth is that you shouldn't put off any detail with Worlds as it is bound to creep up on you before you know it. Working up a week-to-week schedule is extremely important to ensure that you are on top of things.

1. Building your team

It is absolutely vital to secure a team of people who have the trust and respect of one another. Each member should be able to commit a massive amount of time and energy over the next two years. Friends are often lost in the process of running Worlds. So please keep in mind that it is very different from throwing a party with a bunch of your mates. It is very serious work and requires a lot of discipline. Your organizing team should not just understand that principle, but they should ultimately reflect it.

a. The Deputy Chief Adjudicators (DCAs)

The purpose of having a Deputy Chief Adjudicator can be traced back to the 1996 Worlds in Cork. Having just passed the new set of rules, Council decided then that the following Worlds in Stellenbosch would need some oversight in implementing them. John Long (Chief Adjudicator 1996) and Ray D'Cruz (author of Worlds' Rules) served as the very first DCAs.

It has been clear that the DCA has become a largely politicized position. In part, people think that regional/national bias is better served with "one of your own" being named DCA. This is not just unfortunate, but it is patently wrong. The DCA is there to serve as both an external troubleshooter and quality assurance manager. He or she is there to ensure that the motions are closed and fair, that the adjudication panels are balanced, and that the rules are properly upheld.

Getting people with fantastic debating CVs is not as important as getting people who have competent adjudicating CVs. The DCAs should have a solid reputation and the respect of the international debating community. They will be expected to fly out earlier to work with the organizing committee and train the local adjudication pool.

b. Registration Director

This person is accountable for the involvement all of the participants of Worlds. He or she is tasked with sorting out debaters, adjudicators, and observers for each participating institution, ensuring their legitimacy and eligibility. Although all of this work does not start until after the bid is confirmed, it is important to work together a strategy that could be utilized immediately after the bid is confirmed.

Winning a bid will create a surge of interest from every corner of the globe. But you must be able to filter the interested parties from the somewhat-curious-about-this-debating-thing and the dead-set-on-being-there. This person will need to liaise heavily with the Accommodations Director prior to and throughout registration day.

c.   Finance Director

More than just a glorified accountant, this person is responsible for all of the sponsorships, donations, and gifts given to Worlds. Some committees chose to split the job into two roles, finance and marketing. Others kept it as one person to ensure that the money being spent actually existed. This person should always get everything in writing. Records of contracts, letters of intent/support, and receipts should be safely copied and kept.

d.   Tab Director

There is a specific code that needs to be protected during the tournament. This person should not only be an expert with computers and large quantities of data, but needs a clear understanding of how that code relates to running an effective tournament. In other words, you could get an IT genius who never debated before in his life, but he should know the Worlds Constitution Tabulation Article by heart. Even though it may hopefully never be necessary, he should also know how to run a manual tab.

Additionally, this person will need to liaise with the Adjudication Team and should be flexible with their advice. It is not required for an organizing committee to construct its own tab program given the existence of several excellent ones used at past Worlds. The Singapore 2004 Tab was designated as the "official" tab by Council, but it is dependent on compatible hardware.

e.   Contingency Director

Often referred to as the worrywort of the team, this person serves as the internal troubleshooter and quality assurance manager of the entire event. He or she should develop alternative plans for even the most extreme of circumstances. The Contingency Director should sit in at almost every meeting held by each Director.

f.   Equity/Women's Officers

Although Council has a very specific code of conduct and an Equity Officer on the Executive, it is important to have an Organizing Committee Equity Officer to deal with all issues pertaining to conduct. The sensitive nature of this position requires this person to be extremely fair, trustworthy, and decisive.

g.   Accommodations Director

This person is responsible for securing a proper location to house all of the participants, organizing committee, and other guests. He or she should map out all area police stations, hospitals, embassies, restaurants, transit stations, and other places of interest. Some Worlds utilized 24-hour help desks with first-aid kits, emergency contacts, and other vital information. The Accommodations Director will liaise with the Registration Director, the Hotel Manager/Student Residence Manager, and the Contingency Director to meet the lodging needs of the participants. The Accommodations Director must also secure the availability of kosher, halal, vegan, vegetarian, and any other special dietary requirements for all participants.

h.   Event Directors

In addition to the main tournament, Worlds features the World Masters Championship, the World Public Speaking Championship, the World Stand-Up Comedy Competition, and the World Council, Women's & Developing Nations meetings. Each event should have a person in charge, determining the proper location, paraphernalia, and logistics to ensure that everything runs smoothly. The events have very specific requirements and need the requisite coordination.

i.   Communication Director

This person must have the ability to keep consistent correspondence internally and externally from the start until the end of the event. He or she should maintain the website and be connected to all of the appropriate listservs. The Communication Director has to develop a system to ensure that all of the information is duly passed from and to the right parties. They also should be in contact with national and regional media services.

j.   Logistics Director

Anyone who has ever run Worlds before will tell you that volunteers are the lifeblood of an effective event. This person is in charge of the recruitment, training, and deployment of the army of people needed to make this whole thing work. He or she also needs to work out the physical details of each classroom, lecture hall, and campus facility used. The Logistics Director coordinates the room reservations and equipment requirements to ensure a secure environment for the tournament.

k.   Transport Director

From the air/bus/train terminal arrival to the eventual departure, Worlds will depend on this person to make sure that all people can get to where they need to be. The coordination necessary to allow for traffic and weather conditions and mapping out routes to all venues will often be the difference between running a smooth tournament and sheer disaster. Delegates should never be stranded nor should they lack access to sensible transportation alternatives. All transport within the tournament events should be included as part of the expenses.

1.   Socials Director

As much as this might seem to be the "party person" of the team, the socials director will ironically not have the opportunity to enjoy the fruit of his or her labor. This Director will spend all of his or her time sorting out details like, "Are all people getting the food they signed up for? Is the venue up to code for over 1000 people? Are the delegates being charged for stuff we paid for? Are the bouncers turning our delegates away? Is management going to complain about noise ordinances? Are there local party crashers present?"

2.   Work out the details

There are two simple rules to follow: Expect the unexpected and get it in writing. Many of the headaches that past organizers have faced surfaced in the most inopportune time. Attention to detail should come in the planning stage and not during its execution. Schedule the entire event from beginning to end and account for every single hour of every single day. Hear out all of the ideas and work through the alternatives. This is where you have to assume the worst.

Don't depend on a situation unless you have scouted and sourced it out yourselves. You must be able to visualize the angles of everything falling apart and determine how you will come out of it. The team that you just built has to learn how to trust one another. Spend a couple of sessions early on just getting to know each other with team building exercises.

3.   Defend the Bid

You have a year to firm up all of the promises you laid out during the bid presentation. Now is the best time that you will have to start tweaking the bid in spots where you have had the most criticism. Don't spend time trying to spin the circumstances and rationalize errors in early judgement. Take the criticism and see if a correction can be made at this point in time.

a.   The Mid-Year Report

In the July of the year before your bid confirmation, you should send a progress report to the World Council Chair. He or she will first help you determine weak spots in the report and then spread it to the rest of the executive and others interested in your developments. They will have the ability to let you know about where they feel you need help and spot trouble areas.

b.   The ratification process

By October, you should send a Ratification Report to the Council Chair. This will give the Worlds Executive the ability to see the further progress and firm up the Council support by ratifying the bid. The final preparations should continue for the bid confirmation at the Council meeting in January.

4. Future host's night

This event is held at the Worlds prior to yours. This is the best opportunity for you to promote your event, institution, and country. You should work through the details with the organizers of the current Worlds. This is a great opportunity for you to establish connections with the potential delegates to your Worlds. You will need to bring a lot of business cards and contact information.

III. WE HAVE OVER A THOUSAND PEOPLE AT OUR DOORSTEP. WHAT HAPPENS NOW?

Once the bid confirmation is done and you have recovered from Worlds, you have to switch gears for the homestretch. You have the plan and all of the details of your work cut out for you.

1. Execute the plan (Get enough sleep)

The plan should be organized into three time frames: the pre-registration period, the registration period, and the event period. The pre-registration period is rather delicate. This is the first time when you will experience the care necessary in getting the right information at the right time.

Your website should be re-created to include the pre-registration section. It would be smart to require a nominal fee from each participant early on (usually the July prior to your Worlds). This should be collected with the clear caveat that this will not guarantee eligibility for the debaters they field, merely slots for participants. This will give you an early glimpse of what you should expect coming in.

It is recommended that you allot more time for the registration period to begin. The October–November period is best. This will allow for teams to sort out all of their own details and get the payments to you. Doing it too early will make things much easier for you (i.e., you will have the registration fees to work with) but it might be a little unrealistic to expect teams to organize themselves fully by June.

When Worlds rolls around, make sure that you stick to your plan as much as possible. If you need to make changes, do so with your entire team on board. Communication between you and your team as well as the delegates is paramount to running a successful event. Work hard, but don't burn yourself out. Get ample sleep—you are going to need it.

2.   Trust your team (Don't micromanage)

You are a part of a team for a reason. Delegation and trust will help you keep your sanity. More important, the last thing you want to happen is to be involved in the minutiae that a volunteer could have taken care of. You have good people. Let them be good at what they do. Support their decisions as long as the major issues and conditions for Worlds are unaffected.

Keep calm in dealing with the problems that come your way. Yelling at your team will never help. Yelling at the delegates is even worse. And yes, that has been done. This should never be an option for you. Grace under pressure is a contagious attitude. Lead by example.

3.   Passing the gavel (It is done)

I hope that this guide will help you put together the most excellent event of your lifetime. Bidding, planning, and running Worlds will be an endeavor that will inevitably change your life and lives of the debaters, adjudicators, observers, organizers, and volunteers who look part. With all of your hard work, you will win the respect of the entire World.

And who knows, you might end up having fun in the process.

Index